"With over 30 years of experience in education, you learn to recogr a difference in your teaching. *The Success Criteria Playbook* is one developing high-quality success criteria, John Almarode, Douglas Fisher, Kateri Thunder, and Nancy Frey take success criteria to the next level by laying out a step-by-step process that helps teachers ensure every student has clarity and can be successful in meeting the learning intentions. Each module walks you through the process of developing success criteria that help break down barriers and maximize student learning. This book is a must-have in providing your students a clear understanding of what success looks like!"

Barbara J. Lane
Curriculum Coordinator and K–12 Coordinator
San Bernardino County Superintendent of Schools
San Bernardino, CA

"Educators, this book is your next MUST-READ whether you are just hearing about success criteria for the first time or are looking to hone your students' abilities to articulate how they will know they have mastered your learning intentions. *The Success Criteria Playbook* is ideal for engaging in collaborative reflection through PLCs or personal reflection as you seek to make learning visible to your students. With a focus on equity in learning for all students, including those participating in distance learning, this book could not be more relevant to schools today."

Kathryn Campbell
Teacher
Hanover County Public Schools
Mechanicsville, VA

"Not sure how to know if your students are learning? Wondering if your students even know what success looks like for your lessons? *The Success Criteria Playbook: A Hands-On Guide to Making Learning Visible and Measurable* has your answers and more! As a classroom teacher it can be hard to know if your students are learning. It's even harder to know how to adjust for differing assignments, tasks, projects, and evolving expectations. Not all learning is the same, and this book offers clear, teacher-friendly examples that I could immediately take and apply to my own classroom, in whatever scenario I found myself. This book offers wonderful examples from real classrooms that made visualizing this in my own classroom effortless. I was able to easily transfer this text into reality in my classroom. My students know what we are learning, but more importantly they know when they've got it, and those lightbulb moments are what it's all about!"

Christen Wenger
Third-Grade Teacher
Rockingham County Public Schools
Rockingham, VA

"From classroom, school, and district implementation, *The Success Criteria Playbook* provides guidance to navigating the hub for all aspects of quality teaching and learning. John Almarode, Douglas Fisher, Kateri Thunder, and Nancy Frey provide the foundation for developing scaffolded tasks and assessments while incorporating opportunities for feedback. This publication is a hands-on, practical compilation of realistic experience gleaned from classrooms across the world. Standard deconstruction and lesson planning processes start with success criteria. Keys to every learner knowing what they are learning, knowing where they are in their learning, and knowing where they ultimately need to be are found here. *The Success Criteria Playbook* is a true game-changer!"

Josh Maples
Vice Principal
Barren County Public Schools
Glasgow, KY

THE
SUCCESS CRITERIA
PLAYBOOK

GRADES K-12

THE
SUCCESS CRITERIA
PLAYBOOK

A Hands-On Guide to Making Learning Visible and Measurable

Grades K–12

JOHN ALMARODE
DOUGLAS FISHER
KATERI THUNDER
AND NANCY FREY

Sketchnotes by Taryl Hansen

CORWIN
Fisher & Frey

For information:

Corwin
A SAGE Company
2455 Teller Road
Thousand Oaks, California 91320
(800) 233–9936
www.corwin.com

SAGE Publications Ltd.
1 Oliver's Yard
55 City Road
London, EC1Y 1SP
United Kingdom

SAGE Publications India Pvt. Ltd.
B 1/I 1 Mohan Cooperative Industrial Area
Mathura Road, New Delhi 110 044
India

SAGE Publications Asia-Pacific Pte. Ltd.
18 Cross Street #10–10/11/12
China Square Central
Singapore 048423

Printed in the United States of America.

ISBN 9781071831540 (spiral)

Director and Publisher, Corwin Classroom:
    Lisa Luedeke
Editorial Development Manager: Julie Nemer
Associate Content Development Editor:
    Sharon Wu
Production Editor: Tori Mirsadjadi
Copy Editor: Christina West
Typesetter: Integra
Proofreader: Sarah J. Duffy
Indexer: Integra
Cover Designer & Illustrator: Taryl Hanson
Interior Designer: Gail Buschman
Marketing Manager: Deena Meyer

This book is printed on acid-free paper.

23 24 25 10

CONTENTS

PART 3

Visit the companion website at
resources.corwin.com/successcriteriaplaybook
for downloadable resources.

ACKNOWLEDGMENTS

PUBLISHER'S ACKNOWLEDGMENTS

Corwin gratefully acknowledges the contributions of the following reviewers:

Sara Delano Moore
Educator
ORIGO Education
Kent, OH

Kevin Dykema
Teacher
Mattawan Middle School
Mattawan, MI

Brandi Sheppy
Associate Principal
Chula Vista Elementary School District
Chula Vista, CA

Joyce Tugel
STEM Education Consultant
Barrington, NH

Ashley Vasquez
Principal
Chula Vista Elementary School District
Chula Vista, CA

INTRODUCTION

Hitting a target you cannot see is extremely difficult—challenging at best. What would you do if someone asked you to prepare a healthy dinner? Although you know exactly what the intention is, without a clearer description of what this individual means by a healthy dinner, you would likely succeed in meeting that intention if, and only if, you and this person share a common understanding of a healthy dinner. Without that understanding, your success is left to chance. During the planning and preparation, you are left guessing about the ingredients, supplies, and how to use them to create the final product. Without additional information, you would have to wait until the actual presentation of the dinner to even find out if you met expectations.

Now, imagine a similar scenario involving 30 students and a teacher who asks them to construct a viable mathematical argument, gather compelling scientific evidence, use text features to make meaning, or compare two historical accounts of the same event. Without any additional information, these 30 students—much like you and your preparation of a healthy dinner—are left to interpret what is meant by a viable argument, compelling evidence, text features, or an appropriate comparison. The students are clear about the goal or intention (e.g., construct a viable mathematical argument), but their success at meeting the learning intention is left to chance. Ambiguity in expectations of what success looks like in any process, task, or product diminishes learning. This effect applies to both students and teachers (see Table I.1).

> Ambiguity in expectations of what success looks like in any process, task, or product diminishes learning.

TABLE I.1 Ambiguity in Expectations of Success Affects Both Students and Teachers

STUDENTS ARE LIMITED IN THEIR POTENTIAL TO . . .	TEACHERS ARE LIMITED IN THEIR POTENTIAL TO . . .
Retrieve the necessary background knowledge and prior knowledge	Activate the necessary background knowledge and prior knowledge
Identify the necessary tools and skills	Select high-impact approaches or strategies
Monitor their progress toward successful completion	Design and implement checks for understanding that monitor learners' progress
Seek support and feedback	Scaffold and provide feedback to learners
Recognize when they are successful	Decide when learners are ready to move forward

Ensuring that teachers and learners have clarity about expectations through high-quality success criteria increases the likelihood that learning will happen and *all* learners will meet the learning intentions. Thus, we focuses on this critical need. Clarity for learning must move beyond just learning intentions and provide supporting, high-quality success criteria that define what success looks like for *each and every* learner in our schools and classrooms.

Success criteria provide the parameters that establish what success looks like for the learning intentions that day. In our dinner example, success criteria would have provided clear parameters about what a healthy dinner was or was not. Success criteria would also have provided parameters for what makes an argument viable in mathematics, what makes evidence compelling in science, what it means to effectively use text textures, or what is an appropriate comparison of bias in historical documents. This very essential component of teaching and learning is vital in both face-to-face and remote learning environments. Whether teaching and learning are happening in the brick-and-mortar classroom or through a learning management system (LMS), success criteria are necessary for providing a clear view of what success looks like for any process, task, or product.

> Success criteria provide the parameters that establish what success looks like for the learning intentions that day.

To be clear, this is not a new idea nor do we pretend that we are all not at least familiar with success criteria in the classroom. The term *success criteria* has appeared in classrooms and conversations around learning as far back as the late 1950s. In 1968, Paul Harmon defined success criteria as a necessary component of any performance objective associated with student outcomes. He stated that a performance objective must be accompanied by "a paragraph describing the *success criteria* by which student's behavior is to be judged as acceptable or unacceptable" (p. 85). What is most fascinating—and relevant to our discussion here—is that Harmon follows his definition with, you guessed it, a set of parameters that defined quality success criteria. In other words, he provided success criteria for what makes good success criteria. He expected that

> the paragraph will detail, if relevant:
>
> a. the time allowed to complete the performance;
> b. the number, percentage or proportion of total test items that must be answered correctly to pass;
> c. the actual responses that will be considered acceptable;
> d. the person who will judge or evaluate the performance; and
> e. the distinct point in time at which the performance is considered acceptably completed. (Harmon, 1968, p. 85)

Although we have come a long way from this conceptualization of success criteria, you likely have noticed that some challenges arise with the creation and implementation of criteria for success in your own classroom.

We agree. In our work with schools and classrooms around the world, our experiences with classroom walk-throughs, PLC+ professional learning community meetings, and coaching sessions with instructional leaders, teachers, and students suggest that something is not working in our quest to ensure that both we and our learners know what success looks like.

Cathy Youell, a veteran and master elementary teacher, shared feedback with John about this exact concern. Through conversations during grade-level and PLC+ meetings, Cathy noted that her learners continually struggle with answering the question *How will I know that I have learned it?* In most cases, they simply did not answer the question or gave a default response: "When my teacher says so."

Kateri hears this same reflection from teachers. They have practiced setting learning intentions, but describing what it looks and sounds like when students have met those learning intentions is an intimidating challenge. Teachers wonder how to make success criteria specific enough to be measurable while broad enough to allow for student voice and choice. Teachers want to address the "so what" element of learning, but they are not always sure themselves why the content matters beyond their current grade level or outside of school. Doug and Nancy also noticed a decrease in the percentage of learners who could answer this exact question during their classroom visits (Table I.2).

TABLE I.2 Responses to Questions About Learning

	PERCENTAGE OF RESPONSES							
	WEEK OF 10/18	WEEK OF 11/1	WEEK OF 11/8	WEEK OF 11/15	WEEK OF 11/22	WEEK OF 12/6	WEEK OF 12/13	WEEK OF 1/10
What am I learning?	80	80	75	60	75	80	80	85
Why am I learning this?	75	60	65	65	65	70	70	70
How will I know that I have learned it?	50	55	70	60	55	65	65	70

Before we move forward in this playbook, let's do a preassessment to see where you and your learners are in describing *how* they will know if they have learned the information. Using an entrance ticket, one-on-one conferencing, or a computer-based survey (e.g., Mentimeter, Google form), ask your learners the following question: *How will you know that you have learned the information or met the day's success criteria?* Use the space below to summarize their responses and your reflections about their responses.

What percentage of your learners could answer this question? What trends did you notice in the responses? Hold on to these data, and we will revisit this question again in an upcoming module.

Learners appear to struggle when asked to describe *how* they will know if they have learned the information. Through our work in schools and classrooms across the globe, we have found that this struggle differentially affects learners with certain background or demographic characteristics. For example, English language learners may struggle to describe how they know if they have learned the information because of how we create and implement success criteria. How we create and implement success criteria may inadvertently narrow the access and opportunity for learners with a disability to demonstrate their learning progress. If success criteria should provide both the teacher and the learners with a clear understanding of what success looks like, the evidence suggests we are falling short with all learners. Success criteria have an average effect size of 0.88 (Visible Learning Meta[X], 2020). Falling short on providing learners with a clear understanding of what success looks like eliminates the potential to double the rate of learning in our classrooms, which therefore limits the access and opportunity for *all* of our learners to meet the day's learning intentions.

The difficulty our learners have recognizing and articulating criteria for success may be a reflection of our struggle with developing and using success criteria in our classroom. Addressing this struggle is the goal of this playbook. How can we better approach the creation and implementation of success criteria to ensure we and our learners know what success looks like? The answers to this question lie in the modules of this playbook.

THE PURPOSE OF THIS PLAYBOOK

The purpose of this playbook is to take a closer look at the creation and implementation of success criteria so that we can better connect our learners to a shared understanding of what success looks like for any given learning intention. The potential to maximize student learning with success criteria can only be actualized through effective implementation. The modules of this playbook will focus on expanding our understanding of what success criteria are and how we can better utilize them. In addition, we will explore how to better engage our learners in success criteria that lead them to self-monitor, self-reflect, and self-evaluate their own learning.

Up to this point, our perspective and use of success criteria has been far too narrow and thus leads to the very challenges highlighted by Ms. Youell and teachers' reflections as well as the walk-through data presented by Doug and Nancy. We will address those challenges so that both you and your learners can clearly describe what successful learning looks like.

THE LEARNING PLAN WITH THE MODULES

This is a playbook and, by definition, contains a collection of tactics and methods used by a team to accomplish a common goal and get things done (Merriam-Webster, 2020b). In the case of this playbook, the common goal is the creation and implementation of high-quality, high-impact success criteria. Therefore, each of the subsequent modules is designed to support your thinking and use of success criteria in your classroom. But the modules are not necessarily intended to be completed in sequential order or all at once. When coaches and their teams go to their playbooks to get things done, they select the plays that best fit the current context or situation. For example, a spread delay offense designed to slow things down in basketball is not a great play to call if your team is down by 5 points with less than 30 seconds to go in the game. Likewise, the modules in this playbook should be utilized by your team when the current context or situation calls for the module. So, what's the plan?

This playbook is divided into three parts (Table I.3). The first part will look at what success criteria are, where they come from, and the purpose for devoting an entire book, or playbook, to this one concept. This involves tackling five of the biggest challenges encountered when creating and implementing success criteria in our teaching. These barriers, as we have discovered in our own work, result in learners struggling to describe *how* they will know if they have learned the information. This has never been more important than today as we capitalize on the many developments in instructional technology to support remote learning. If learners are not physically in a classroom, we must ensure they know what success looks like from a distance. Starting with what success criteria are and where they come from, we will spend time thinking about the role of success criteria in processes, products, and dispositions.

The second part of this playbook takes an up-close look at the variety of options we have in creating and implementing success criteria. From creating *I can* statements to co-constructing success criteria, we will devote individual modules to each of the options we have for helping our learners know what success looks like. From there, we enter the third part of this playbook. This final part focuses on the relationship between high-impact, high-quality success criteria and meta-cognition, deliberate practice, feedback, and equity. We will look at where success criteria come from and how to align our approach to creating and implementing them based on the types of learning expected in the day's lesson. Finally, we will devote considerable attention to the role success criteria play in promoting self-monitoring, self-reflection, and self-evaluation through effective feedback and deliberate practice.

TABLE 1.3 **The Success Criteria Playbook Overview**

		FOCUS
Part 1		
	Module 1	What Are Success Criteria?
	Module 2	What Are the Challenges to Creating and Implementing Success Criteria? How Do We Overcome Those Challenges?
	Module 3	How Do Success Criteria Pave the Way for Equity?
Part 2		
	Modules 4–9	What Is the Continuum of Success Criteria? • *I Can/We Can* Statements (Module 4) • Single-Point Rubrics (Module 5) • Analytic/Holistic Rubrics (Module 6) • Teacher Modeling (Module 7) • Exemplars (Module 8) • Co-Constructing Criteria for Success (Module 9)
	Module 10	Different Types of Success Criteria for Different Aspects of Learning
Part 3		
	Module 11	How Do We Use Success Criteria to Foster Meta-Cognition?
	Module 12	How Do Success Criteria Support Deliberate Practice and Transfer of Learning?
	Module 13	What Is the Relationship Between Success Criteria Feedback?
	Module 14	How Do We Use Success Criteria to Fulfill the Promise of Equity?

For Modules 4–9, you and your PLC+ team members will utilize these when the context of the learning in your classrooms calls for them. Success criteria are important in our quest to develop learners who take ownership of their learning and engage in self-monitoring, self-reflection, and self-evaluation. But the creation and implementation of success criteria can be challenging. Ensuring that our criteria for success are not circular, incorporate more than just procedural learning, include the processes of learning, can be measured, and move beyond *I can* statements requires us to focus on

> High-quality success criteria improve our decisions about teaching and improve the outcomes of our learners.

why we use success criteria to begin with. High-quality success criteria improve our decisions about teaching and improve the outcomes of our learners. So, our hope then is that you will approach this challenge with these benefits in mind. If learners in your classroom are not able to articulate what success looks like or how they know that they have learned it, we hope that you will use Modules 4–9 to rethink your approach through reflective questioning. Here are some examples:

- Do my success criteria truly represent the learning intentions for my learners?
- Did I pick the best option for implementing success criteria based on the type of learning expected of my students?
- Am I using success criteria to support my students taking ownership of their learning?

Expanding our perspective on what success criteria are and how we utilize them in our classrooms will have a noticeable effect on how our learners engage in the learning.

Let's establish your own learning intentions and success criteria for your work in the playbook. What do you want to learn from this playbook (learning intention) and how will you know you have learned it (success criteria)? These can be individual as well as collective learning intentions and success criteria. Use the space provided to record your goals and criteria for success.

Just as you did with your data from the previous task, keep this information close by so that we can revisit these learning intentions and success criteria throughout the playbook.

LEARNING WITHIN THE MODULES

We make two assumptions about your learning journey in this playbook. First, we assume you have used *The Teacher Clarity Playbook, Grades K–12: A Hands-On Guide to Creating Learning Intentions and Success Criteria for Organized, Effective Instruction* (Fisher, Frey, Amador, & Assof, 2019) and are familiar with the processes in that book. Thus, we will not repeat the information about analyzing standards and developing learning progressions. However, those are absolutely necessary and essential skills and understandings for this playbook. This is the next step! Second, we assume that you have noticed that your learners, and maybe even you, struggle with knowing what success looks like in your classroom. This may be evident in the data you collected in the above task. If these two assumptions fit your current professional learning journey, this playbook is for you.

Each of the modules begins with a self-assessment and then introduces a specific goal, an explanation of the ideas within the module to establish the focus for the learning (a learning intention). The module then continues with modeling how the process is applied through examples across learning domains. Examples will cover primary, elementary, middle school, and high school content, skills, practices, dispositions, and understandings. From kindergarten to calculus and from learning to read to writing compelling reports, we seek to provide a wide range of examples to show that high-quality success criteria can serve as a shared language for how we communicate expectations in our classrooms.

Each module offers you an opportunity for practice and application with a variety of content and grade levels. The practice section encourages you to write your answers and discuss them with your team, if possible. Although using this book as part of your personal learning is possible, the creation and implementation of high-quality success criteria is best done collectively with colleagues. One benefit of this collaboration is the opportunity to engage in critical dialogue around what success looks like for you and your learners. These critical conversations will provide feedback on the quality of our criteria.

Each module also includes opportunities for creating and implementing high-quality success criteria that can be used immediately in your classroom. Again, this is best done during collaborative planning or during your PLC+ meeting (Fisher, Frey, Almarode, Flories, & Nagel, 2020). At the end of the modules, you are asked to self-assess. This will allow you to check your own understanding and to identify areas to focus on in the future.

COLLABORATING TO CREATE AND IMPLEMENT HIGH-QUALITY SUCCESS CRITERIA

The most effective way to create and implement high-quality success criteria is to work collaboratively with your grade-level team, content team, or PLC+. We believe that the work of this playbook is an essential component of the work you do in your PLC+. The use of these five guiding questions of PLC+ will keep the focus relentlessly on the learning of our students:

- Where are we going?
- Where are we now?
- How do we move learning forward?
- What did we learn today?
- Who benefited and who did not benefit? (Fisher et al., 2020, p. 8)

In PLC+, teachers identify learning intentions and discuss ideas for instruction. They meet to review student work and figure out if their efforts have been fruitful. They also talk about students who need additional instruction or intervention to be successful. This is all informed and supported by high-quality success criteria. High-quality success criteria ensure that we have high expectations, focus on a common understanding of what success looks like, activate the conversation around learning, and ensure equity of access and opportunity to learning for all students (Table I.4).

TABLE I.4 How Success Criteria Support the Work of PLC+

PLC QUESTION	TEACHER CLARITY MODULE	DESCRIPTION
Where are we going?	Modules 4–9: What Is the Continuum of Success Criteria? ◦ *I Can/We Can* Statements (Module 4) ◦ Single-Point Rubrics (Module 5) ◦ Analytic/Holistic Rubrics (Module 6) ◦ Teacher Modeling (Module 7) ◦ Exemplars (Module 8) ◦ Co-Constructing Criteria for Success (Module 9)	These modules focus on what success criteria are and are not. This includes looking at the different approaches for creating and implementing success criteria.
Where are we now?	Module 10: Different Types of Success Criteria for Different Aspects of Learning Module 11: How Do We Use Success Criteria to Foster Meta-Cognition?	Knowing where learners are requires that both teachers and learners know their current level of understanding. Success criteria provide that clarity to both teachers and learners.
How do we move learning forward?	Module 11: How Do We Use Success Criteria to Foster Meta-Cognition? Module 12: How Do Success Criteria Support Deliberate Practice and Transfer of Learning? Module 13: What Is The Relationship Between Success Criteria and Feedback?	To address this question, we have to leverage the high-quality success criteria to engage learners in taking ownership of their learning, engage in deliberate practice, and give and receive feedback.

CONTINUED

CONTINUED

PLC QUESTION	TEACHER CLARITY MODULE	DESCRIPTION
What did we learn today?	• Module 12: How Do Success Criteria Support Deliberate Practice and Transfer of Learning? • Module 13: What Is the Relationship Between Success Criteria and Feedback?	These modules look at how success criteria give insight into providing opportunities for learners to practice. These practice opportunities allow for the giving and receiving of feedback about learners' progress and our teaching.
Who benefited and who did not benefit?	• Module 12: How Do Success Criteria Support Deliberate Practice and Transfer of Learning? • Module 14: How Do We Use Success Criteria to Fulfill the Promise of Equity?	These modules ensure that all learners have access and opportunity to high-quality teaching and learning. Success criteria set the high expectations for this to occur. Specifically in Module 14, we look at how to ensure equity in our classrooms.

 Available for download at **resources.corwin.com/successcriteriaplaybook**

Now, let's get started!

PART 1

MODULE 1
WHAT ARE SUCCESS CRITERIA?

Before you engage with the information in this module, rate yourself on each of the following success criteria using the four-item scale:

- I can define success criteria.

  Novice > Apprentice > Practitioner > Expert

- I can explain the relationship between success criteria and learning intentions.

  Novice > Apprentice > Practitioner > Expert

- I can explain the difference between content, practice, and dispositional success criteria.

  Novice > Apprentice > Practitioner > Expert

- I can develop a list of what learners would say and do to demonstrate success for content, practices, and dispositions.

  Novice > Apprentice > Practitioner > Expert

You'll use these definitions throughout this playbook:

- **Novice:** I am just starting to learn this, and I don't really understand it yet.
- **Apprentice:** I am starting to get it, but I still need someone to coach me.
- **Practitioner:** I understand it well or can do it myself but sometimes I get stuck.
- **Expert:** I understand it well and can teach others.

Let's return to our examples of learning intentions from the Introduction:

- Construct a viable mathematical argument
- Gather compelling scientific evidence
- Use text features to make meaning
- Compare two historical accounts of the same event

What if there was additional information to accompany these statements? Of the following options, which ones might offer the additional clarity that learners need to understand what is expected of them and that the teacher needs to be able to monitor student progress? Which of the three options for each statement enhances clarity around what success looks like for learners?

LEARNING INTENTION	OPTION 1	OPTION 2	OPTION 3
Construct a viable mathematical argument	The teacher provides three video clips of learners constructing viable mathematical arguments and narrates these clips showing her learners the reasons that these are considered an exemplar.	Students are provided several examples and non-examples and are tasked with developing the "essential characteristics" of a viable mathematical argument.	The teacher provides his learners with a single-point rubric that allows them to self-evaluate their argument and get feedback from him.
Gather compelling scientific evidence	The teacher provides his learners with a checklist of look-fors that support learners in evaluating the nature of the scientific evidence they are gathering.	During a demonstration, the teacher models her thinking using a think-aloud protocol to make decisions about whether evidence is compelling or not.	The teacher provides a series of *I can* statements that break down the steps needed to gather compelling scientific evidence.
Use text features to make meaning	The teacher provides a set of *We can* statements for learners at the literacy center.	The teacher provides a video that shows her using text features that is available asynchronously on the class website.	The teacher provides an exemplar and walks her learners through the reasons that this is considered an exemplar.
Compare two historical accounts of the same event	The teacher provides a checklist of components to consider when analyzing bias and writing an effective comparison.	The teacher provides a rubric that scales proficiency on five different indicators that have been taught to students regarding comparisons of historical documents.	The teacher meets with groups of students to develop indicators of success based on the mentor texts students have read.

You likely circled all the options. They all provide more clarity about what success looks like than the original statements. But why? Before moving on, take a moment to list the common characteristics of the options you selected. Why did they provide you with additional clarity and why do you think they would provide additional clarity for your learners?

The additional options share similar characteristics. They all do the following:

- Provide a path for learners to meet the expectations.
- Include multiple steps leading to successful learning (i.e., not just a single criterion for success; reasons, characteristics, components, indicators, look-fors, decisions, and statements are all plural).
- Allow the teacher to monitor learners' progress toward those expectations.
- Help learners answer the question: How will I know that I have learned it?
- Help teachers answer the question: How will I know that they have learned it?

WHAT ARE SUCCESS CRITERIA?

Success criteria should provide a clear answer to the question: *How will I know that I have learned it?* or *How will we know that we have learned it?*

> Success criteria should provide a clear answer to the question: *How will I know that I have learned it?* or *How will we know that we have learned it?*

Success criteria make the learning intention, or "it," visible for both teachers and students by describing what learners must know and be able to do that would demonstrate that they have met the learning intentions for the day. However, describing success for a task like constructing a viable mathematical argument, gathering compelling evidence, using text features to make meaning, or comparing historical accounts of the same event requires more than just a single "know" or "do." Multiple components are involved in each of these complex learning intentions. This means that each intention has multiple criteria for success that outline the

path necessary for demonstrating mastery of the learning. For learners, these success criteria provide clarity around their expected learning progression toward the desired outcomes of the learning experience. Whether students are engaged in face-to-face or remote learning, success criteria allow them to see what they will be expected to say and do to demonstrate their learning and, eventually, self-monitor, self-reflect, and self-evaluate their work toward that end. For teachers, success criteria provide details that allow us to monitor our students' progress in their learning journey. We must have multiple checkpoints along the way to ensure that all learners are making progress toward the learning intention.

Success criteria bridge the gap between the learning intentions of the teacher and the level of active engagement required of the learner to meet those expectations. Students need to know not just what they are expected to learn, but also *how* they will demonstrate that they know it. Knowing the *how* supports learners as they

- retrieve background and prior knowledge,
- identify the necessary tools to engage in the learning,
- monitor their progress,
- seek feedback,
- recognize when they have met the learning intention.

Teachers, then, can implement specific strategies that

- activate that background knowledge,
- ensure meaningful learning experiences in face-to-face or virtual environments,
- monitor learners' progress,
- provide feedback,
- recognize when learners need additional support or are ready to move forward in their learning.

High-quality success criteria not only make the learning intention visible; success criteria *define* the learning intention (Figure 1.1). Success criteria *define* the target.

High-quality success criteria not only make the learning intention visible; success criteria *define* the learning intention.

FIGURE 1.1 Success Criteria Define the Learning Intention

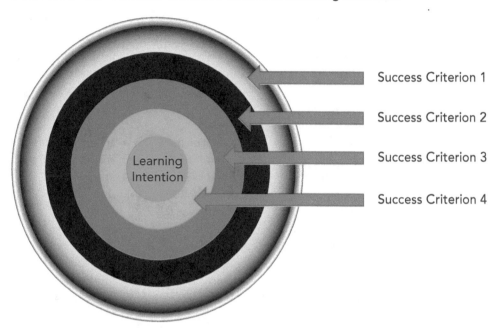

LAYING THE GROUNDWORK FOR DEVELOPING HIGH-QUALITY SUCCESS CRITERIA

The careful unpacking and analysis of standards allows us to generate learning intentions. Success criteria come from deconstructing those learning intentions into measurable and actionable elements that, when considered together, clarify what it means to successfully meet the learning intentions. The process for developing success criteria starts with us first answering the following reflective question with our colleagues:

> *What would learners say and do if they have truly mastered the learning intention?*

The table that follows has examples of how to utilize success criteria to define the targeted learning intention.

	ELEMENTARY MATHEMATICS	BIOLOGY	ELEMENTARY ENGLISH LANGUAGE ARTS	WORLD HISTORY
What is the learning intention?	We are learning about the relationship of equality between two values.	We are learning about the transformation and flow of energy through photosynthesis.	We are learning how text features contribute to the meaning of a text.	We are learning about the causes of the French Revolution.
What would learners say and do if they have mastered the learning intention?	• Name the two values within a mathematical context. • Represent the two values using manipulatives, diagrams, numbers, and words. • Describe the relationship between the two values using a balance scale or number line. • Manipulate or change the two values by adding, subtracting, multiplying, or dividing and yet maintain equality.	• Name the cell parts involved in photosynthesis. • Describe the process of photosynthesis. • Give the chemical equations for photosynthesis. • Describe the role of ATP in the storage and release of chemical energy. • Explain the role of light. • Compare and contrast photosynthesis and cellular respiration.	• Name text features (e.g., graphs, charts). • Extract information from various text features. • Compare information from the text features to the text itself. • Describe the ways in which the information from the text features added to their understanding of the text.	• Recognize the time period. • Describe the international struggle of the time. • Explain the social antagonisms (the aristocracy and the bourgeoisie). • Describe the leadership at the time and the effectiveness of that leader. • Explain the economic hardships within the country.

To fully engage with this playbook, you and your colleagues will need to have full access to your unpacked and analyzed standards of learning and your learning intentions. We will continually refer to these learning intentions as we create and implement success criteria.

GUIDED PRACTICE

For the following learning intentions, describe what learners would say and do if they have mastered the learning intentions. After you and your colleagues have completed the guided practice below, please turn to page 28 for suggested answers. These are only suggested answers, as there are different ways to complete the guided practice.

CONTENT	ELEMENTARY MATHEMATICS	BIOLOGY	ELEMENTARY ENGLISH LANGUAGE ARTS	WORLD HISTORY
What is the learning intention?	We are learning to reason about the values of numbers and to find a reasonable estimate when an exact value is not needed or possible.	We are learning about the relationship between human activities and their impact on the environment.	We are learning to write "how-to" texts that sequence information.	We are learning about responses to capitalism, such as utopianism, social democracy, socialism, and communism.
What would learners say and do if they have mastered the learning intention?				

YOUR TURN!

During your PLC+ or collaborative planning meeting, work with your colleagues to locate several of your upcoming learning intentions in the current or next unit of study. List those in the following table. Then, use the space to the right to respond to the reflective question:

What would learners say and do if they have mastered the learning intention?

CONTENT	TOPIC	TOPIC
What is the learning intention?		
What would learners say and do if they have mastered the learning intention?	1. 2. 3. 4. 5.	1. 2. 3. 4. 5.

CONTENT, PRACTICES, AND DISPOSITIONS

Notice that the examples provided on page 18 focus on the **content** contained with the standards. These learning intentions are not the standards themselves, but the part of the standard that is being taught. Just as there are content learning intentions, social-emotional learning intentions, and language learning intentions (Fisher et al., 2019), there are more ways to define success than just content mastery. Some success criteria focus on **practices** and others on **dispositions**. In the following sections, we will explore these two additional ways to define success.

PRACTICES

Practices, such as the eight Common Core State Standards for Mathematical Practices (National Governors Association Center for Best Practices & Council of Chief State School Officers, 2010) or eight Science and Engineering Practices (National Research Council, 2013), can be integrated into student learning.

COMMON CORE STATE STANDARDS FOR MATHEMATICAL PRACTICES	SCIENCE AND ENGINEERING PRACTICES
1. Make sense of problems and persevere in solving them. 2. Reason abstractly and quantitatively. 3. Construct viable arguments and critique the reasoning of others. 4. Model with mathematics 5. Use appropriate tools strategically. 6. Attend to precision. 7. Look for and make use of structure. 8. Look for and express regularity in repeated reasoning.	1. Asking questions (for science) and defining problems (for engineering). 2. Developing and using models. 3. Planning and carrying out investigations. 4. Analyzing and interpreting data. 5. Using mathematics and computational thinking. 6. Constructing explanations (for science) and designing solutions (for engineering). 7. Engaging in argument from evidence. 8. Obtaining, evaluating, and communicating information.

Sources: National Governors Association Center for Best Practices & Council of Chief State School Officers (2010); National Research Council (2013).

Similarly, some states have processes that transcend grade levels. In California, for example, students in Grades K–5 are expected to develop the following Historical and Social Sciences Analysis Skills (note that the same three categories exist for adolescents but the content is different):

Chronological and Spatial Thinking

1. Students place key events and people of the historical era they are studying in a chronological sequence and within a spatial context; they interpret timelines.

2. Students correctly apply terms related to time, including *past, present, future, decade, century,* and *generation.*

3. Students explain how the present is connected to the past, identifying both similarities and differences between the two, and how some things change over time and some things stay the same.

4. Students use map and globe skills to determine the absolute locations of places and interpret information available through a map's or globe's legend, scale, and symbolic representations.

5. Students judge the significance of the relative location of a place (e.g., proximity to a harbor, on trade routes) and analyze how relative advantages or disadvantages can change over time.

Research, Evidence, and Point of View

1. Students differentiate between primary and secondary sources.

2. Students pose relevant questions about events they encounter in historical documents, eyewitness accounts, oral histories, letters, diaries, artifacts, photographs, maps, artworks, and architecture.

3. Students distinguish fact from fiction by comparing documentary sources on historical figures and events with fictionalized characters and events.

Historical Interpretation

1. Students summarize the key events of the era they are studying and explain the historical contexts of those events.

2. Students identify the human and physical characteristics of the places they are studying and explain how those features form the unique character of those places.

3. Students identify and interpret the multiple causes and effects of historical events.

4. Students conduct cost-benefit analyses of historical and current events. (California Department of Education, 2019)

In Florida, the following processes are expected of students in English language arts across all grade levels:

- Cite evidence to explain and justify reasoning.

- Read and comprehend grade-level complex texts proficiently.

- Make inferences to support comprehension.

- Use appropriate collaborative techniques and active listening skills when engaging in discussions in a variety of situations.

- Use the accepted rules governing a specific format to create quality work.

- Use appropriate voice and tone when speaking or writing. (Florida Department of Education, 2019)

When appropriate to grade level, subject, and location, we should incorporate these practices into what learners would say and do if they mastered the learning intention.

PRACTICES	ELEMENTARY MATHEMATICS	BIOLOGY	ELEMENTARY ENGLISH LANGUAGE ARTS	WORLD HISTORY
What is the learning intention?	We are learning about the relationship of equality between two values.	We are learning about the transformation and flow of energy through photosynthesis.	We are learning how text features contribute to the meaning of a text.	We are learning about the causes of the French Revolution.
What would learners say and do if they have mastered the learning intention?	• Explain the relationship of equality between the two values using the meaning of the equal sign (phrases like *same as*) and multiple representations of the values.	• Use a model based on evidence to illustrate the relationships between systems or between components of a system.	• Make inferences from the text features. • Talk with peers about the text features and their contributions to the understanding of the text.	• Identify bias and prejudice in historical interpretations. • Show the connections, causal and otherwise, between particular historical events and larger social, economic, and political trends and developments.

GUIDED PRACTICE

For the following learning intentions, describe what learners would say and do if they have mastered the learning intentions. After you and your colleagues have completed the guided practice below, please turn to page 28 for suggested answers. These are only suggested answers, as there are different ways to complete the guided practice.

PRACTICES	ELEMENTARY MATHEMATICS	BIOLOGY	ELEMENTARY ENGLISH LANGUAGE ARTS	WORLD HISTORY
What is the learning intention?	We are learning to reason about the values of numbers and to find a reasonable estimate when an exact value is not needed or possible.	We are learning about the relationship between human activities and their impact on the environment.	We are learning to write "how-to" texts that sequence information.	We are learning about responses to capitalism, such as utopianism, social democracy, socialism, and communism.
What would learners say and do if they have mastered the learning intention?				

YOUR TURN!

Return to the work of you and your colleagues on page 20. In addition to the content, what **practices** would you expect to see from learners who have mastered the learning intention? Add those practices to the table on page 20.

DISPOSITIONS

Dispositions are ways in which learners approach and engage in learning. One way of thinking about dispositions is as predominant tendencies we want learners to have when they engage in life-long learning. Dispositions move beyond specific practices in mathematics, science, English language arts, or social studies and encompass the natural inclinations of our learners when they engage in new learning. These dispositions might be the focus of a school-wide initiative on what it means to be a good learner in your particular school or a list of dispositions you and your colleagues want to build and support in your learners. Examples of dispositions include the following:

- Critical thinking
- Communication
- Creativity

- Curiosity
- Perseverance
- Confidence
- Responsibility
- Collaboration
-
-
-

Are there any dispositions you and your colleagues seek to build and support in your learners? What does it mean to be a good learner at your school? Please add those dispositions to the list.

Looking one last time to the four examples we started with on page 18, here are examples of dispositions that these teachers want to instill in their learners.

DISPOSITIONS	ELEMENTARY MATHEMATICS	BIOLOGY	ELEMENTARY ENGLISH LANGUAGE ARTS	WORLD HISTORY
What is the learning intention?	We are learning about the relationship of equality between two values.	We are learning about the transformation and flow of energy through photosynthesis.	We are learning how text features contribute to the meaning of a text.	We are learning about the causes of the French Revolution.
What would learners say and do if they have mastered the learning intention?	• Compare what is similar and different between their own representations and reasoning and their classmates'.	• Communicate how photosynthesis converts light energy into chemical energy through discourse with peers.	• Monitor their emotional response when they are not sure that they are right.	• Take responsibility for their learning and the learning of their team.

These dispositions integrate language and social-emotional learning outcomes into the success criteria.

GUIDED PRACTICE

For the following learning intentions, describe what dispositions you and your colleagues would like learners to develop through this learning. Again, when finished, please turn to page 29 for suggested answers.

DISPOSITIONS	ELEMENTARY MATHEMATICS	BIOLOGY	ELEMENTARY ENGLISH LANGUAGE ARTS	WORLD HISTORY
What is the learning intention?	We are learning to reason about the values of numbers and to find a reasonable estimate when an exact value is not needed or possible.	We are learning about the relationship between human activities and their impact on the environment.	We are learning to write "how-to" texts that sequence information.	We are learning about responses to capitalism, such as utopianism, social democracy, socialism, and communism.
What would learners say and do if they have mastered the learning intention?				

YOUR TURN!

Return to the work of you and your colleagues on page 20. In addition to the content and practices, identify the dispositions you would expect to see from learners who have mastered the learning intention. Add those dispositions to the content and practices you have already listed on page 20.

WHERE TO NEXT?

In this module, we developed a definition of success criteria and explored their role in defining the target and making it visible to both our learners and ourselves. The creation of high-impact, high-quality success criteria is a process that starts with us reflectively thinking about what learners would say and do if they have truly mastered the learning intention. This is not limited to **content** but should also include **practices** and **dispositions** that reflect social-emotional and language learning intentions (Fisher et al., 2019). However, this is just the beginning. Our next module will look at how to take the list you and your colleagues generated on page 20 and begin to think about how to implement success criteria that will define and make the target visible. In other words, how do we move forward from our lists of what learners would be able to say and do and create and implement high-quality success criteria? And what do those success criteria look like?

Now that you have finished this module, rate yourself on each of the following success criteria using the four-item scale. Use the space provided at the end to self-reflect on your own learning. What will you do next with this information? You may not yet be at the expert level, as it takes time to integrate knowledge into practice. Use this information to identify areas of continued learning.

- I can define success criteria.

  Novice > Apprentice > Practitioner > Expert

- I can explain the relationship between success criteria and learning intentions.

  Novice > Apprentice > Practitioner > Expert

- I can explain the difference between content, practice, and dispositional success criteria.

  Novice > Apprentice > Practitioner > Expert

- I can develop a list of what learners would say and do to demonstrate success for content, practices, and dispositions.

  Novice > Apprentice > Practitioner > Expert

SUGGESTED ANSWERS FOR MODULE 1

These "answers" for the Guided Practice sections represent some options among many possible success criteria for the topics and learning intentions. These examples are meant to provide you with feedback as you grow in your understanding and implementation of success criteria. Compare your success criteria with ours. What do you notice?

Perhaps you chose different verbs.

Perhaps you chose to emphasize different pivotal content, practices, or dispositions.

Regardless of these differences, all of our success criteria are created based on the standards and aligned with the learning intentions. Your success criteria and ours should share the following essential characteristics of success criteria:

- Provide a path for learners to meet the expectations.

- Include multiple steps leading to successful learning (i.e., not just a single criterion for success; reasons, characteristics, components, indicators, look-fors, decisions, and statements are all plural).

- Allow the teacher to monitor learners' progress toward those expectations.

- Help learners answer the question: How will I know that I have learned it?

- Help teachers answer the question: How will I know that they have learned it?

Your decisions about what to include in success criteria may depend on your grade level, the readiness and interests of your learners, the specific strengths and needs of your learners, and where you are within the sequence of your unit and school year. You know your learners best. As you make decisions to create success criteria, draw on this expertise. Then, use feedback from your learners to make adjustments and refine the way you phrase, show, and engage learners with success criteria.

CONTENT	ELEMENTARY MATHEMATICS	BIOLOGY	ELEMENTARY ENGLISH LANGUAGE ARTS	WORLD HISTORY
What is the learning intention?	We are learning to reason about the values of numbers and to find a reasonable estimate when an exact value is not needed or possible.	We are learning about the relationship between human activities and their impact on the environment.	We are learning to write "how-to" texts that sequence information.	We are learning about responses to capitalism, such as utopianism, social democracy, socialism, and communism.
What would learners say and do if they have mastered the learning intention?	• Describe an estimate using language such as *about, between, more than, less than,* or *a little more/less than.* • Explain the reasonableness of the estimate using a benchmark (place value, compatible numbers) as a reference.	• Provide examples to illustrate and explain how habitat destruction, pollution, introduction of invasive species, overexploitation, and climate change can disrupt an ecosystem and threaten the survival of species.	• List information in order so that the reader knows the right steps. • Include details in each step that are descriptive.	• Define each term. • Compare each to capitalism.

PRACTICES	ELEMENTARY MATHEMATICS	BIOLOGY	ELEMENTARY ENGLISH LANGUAGE ARTS	WORLD HISTORY
What is the learning intention?	We are learning to reason about the values of numbers and to find a reasonable estimate when an exact value is not needed or possible.	We are learning about the relationship between human activities and their impact on the environment.	We are learning to write "how-to" texts that sequence information.	We are learning about responses to capitalism, such as utopianism, social democracy, socialism, and communism.
What would learners say and do if they have mastered the learning intention?	• Compare estimates and reasoning with peers' thinking in order to refine estimates.	• Design, evaluate, and refine a solution for reducing the negative effects of human activity on a watershed or ecosystem.	• Read and re-read to determine if steps are missing.	• Identify sources of bias. • Compare and contrast information from different sources.

DISPOSITIONS	ELEMENTARY MATHEMATICS	BIOLOGY	ELEMENTARY ENGLISH LANGUAGE ARTS	WORLD HISTORY
What is the learning intention?	We are learning to reason about the values of numbers and to find a reasonable estimate when an exact value is not needed or possible.	We are learning about the relationship between human activities and their impact on the environment.	We are learning to write "how-to" texts that sequence information.	We are learning about responses to capitalism, such as utopianism, social democracy, socialism, and communism.
What would learners say and do if they have mastered the learning intention?	• Reflect on estimation strategies and select a new strategy to try in a similar situation.	• Work collaboratively to solve an environmental problem caused by human activities. • Use critical thinking in designing, refining, and evaluating a solution for reducing the negative effects of human activity on a watershed or ecosystem.	• Self-assess to determine if the order of items is correct. • Persevere in working through the details required to ensure that the reader could follow the process.	• Suspend personal opinions while learning about other systems. • Organize information clearly to be able to compare.

NOTES

MODULE 2
WHAT ARE THE CHALLENGES TO CREATING AND IMPLEMENTING SUCCESS CRITERIA? HOW DO WE OVERCOME THOSE CHALLENGES?

Before you engage with the information in this module, rate yourself on each of the following success criteria using the four-item scale:

- I can describe challenges associated with creating and implementing success criteria.

- I can explain ways to overcome common challenges associated with creating and implementing success criteria.

- I can list different ways of implementing success criteria.

- I can work with my peers to analyze success criteria.

Describing what we expect learners to say and do if they have met the learning intentions is one thing; sharing that expectation with our learners is something different. We cannot stop at just *us* knowing what success looks like; we have to share this with our students. The transition from learning intentions to the creation and implementation of success criteria has come with unanticipated challenges for many of us. But know that this is a process of continued improvement. Something is better than nothing, so please do not become paralyzed and give up if this is hard work at first. Knowing now what the challenges are will help us overcome them during our work in this playbook and leverage the full potential of success criteria to yield greater student learning.

> We cannot stop at just *us* knowing what success looks like; we have to share this with our students.

Using the data collected in the Introduction (turn back to page 4), what challenges have you encountered in creating and implementing success criteria? Jot down your challenges and the challenges of your colleagues or PLC+. What specific evidence or experiences indicated that these are challenges? In other words, what did you or your learners say and do?

CHALLENGES TO CREATING AND IMPLEMENTING SUCCESS CRITERIA

Let's look at some of the common challenges in creating and implementing success criteria in our schools and classrooms. Many of these may be on your own list of experiences. From data collected through classroom walk-throughs, PLC+ meetings, and coaching sessions with instructional leaders, teachers, and students, we have identified the following challenges:

1. Circular learning intentions and success criteria

2. Too procedural

3. Product-focused

4. Not measurable

5. Agenda or set of directions

As we look closer at how these challenges manifest themselves in the classroom, keep in mind that each module from this point forward is designed to address these challenges. For now, we are just calling them out and providing non-examples of success criteria that exemplify these challenges so that we can better utilize this playbook to address the specific challenges in your school and class.

CHALLENGE 1: CIRCULAR LEARNING INTENTIONS AND SUCCESS CRITERIA

One of the challenges we face in creating and implementing success criteria is the use of circular phrasing between the learning intentions and success criteria. In some classrooms, the learning intention and success criteria are presented as answers to three questions: *What am I learning*? *Why am I learning this*? *How will I know that I have learned it?* In the case of circular phrasing, the learning intention and success criteria are the same thing, thus providing no clear understanding about the learning or the evidence that will demonstrate learning. Let's look at our first set of non-examples of success criteria that exemplify this circular phrasing.

HIGH SCHOOL ALGEBRA: SYSTEMS OF EQUATIONS

What am I learning?	I am learning about solving systems of equations.
Why am I learning this?	So that I can solve systems of equations.
How will I know that I have learned it?	When I can solve systems of equations.

ELEMENTARY SCIENCE: MATTER

What am I learning?	I am learning about the different types of matter.
Why am I learning this?	So that I can know the different types of matter.
How will I know that I have learned it?	When I can identify the different types of matter.

KINDERGARTEN ENGLISH LANGUAGE ARTS: KEY IDEAS AND DETAILS

What am I learning?	I am learning to ask and answer questions about details in a text.
Why am I learning this?	So that I can ask and answer about details in a text.
How will I know that I have learned it?	When I can ask and answer about details in a text.

MIDDLE SCHOOL HISTORY: ANCIENT EGYPT

What am I learning?	I am learning to locate and describe the major river systems and how they supported permanent settlement and early civilizations.
Why am I learning this?	So that I can tell how rivers supported early civilizations.
How will I know that I have learned it?	When I can locate rivers and describe how they supported permanent settlement and civilizations.

Although the success criteria in the examples are visible to both the teacher and the student, this phrasing, and thus logic, is circular. Therefore, these success criteria are not adding to students' understanding of what learning looks like. Take a moment to brainstorm what causes circular phrasing and possible ways to address the challenge. In other words, what could these teachers do to avoid this challenge?

CHALLENGE 2: TOO PROCEDURAL

Another challenge with success criteria is the disproportionate focus on *procedural outcomes*. Solving for the missing variable, writing a descriptive paragraph, calculating the slope, answering the "W" questions, listing a fact family, solving net force equations, naming the three branches of government, balancing chemical equations, and listing the steps of mitosis are all outcomes linked to procedural knowledge. Success criteria can and should incorporate *conceptual learning*, *application of concepts and thinking*, *dispositions*, and *collective or collaborative learning outcomes* (i.e., *I can* versus *We can*). Although incorporating each of these into a single learning experience is equally unrealistic, focusing solely on procedures is a far too limited view of success and quickly turns into simply "getting to the right answer" without understanding that answer.

Success criteria can and should incorporate the following:

- conceptual learning
- application of concepts and thinking
- dispositions
- collective or collaborative learning outcomes

MIDDLE SCHOOL MATHEMATICS: MEASUREMENT AND GEOMETRY

What am I learning?	I am learning that the circumference of a circle is proportional to its diameter.
Why am I learning this?	So that I can understand geometric relationships in circles.
How will I know that I have learned it?	When I can state the value of pi. When I can identify the parts of the equation for circumference. When I can solve for the diameter. When I can find the circumference given *d*. When I can find circumference given *r*.

ELEMENTARY SCIENCE: EARTH AND SPACE SYSTEMS

What am I learning?	I am learning about our solar system.
Why am I learning this?	So that I can understand my place in the universe.
How will I know that I have learned it?	When I can name the eight planets. When I can list them in order from closest to farthest from the sun.

ENGLISH LANGUAGE ARTS: FOUNDATIONAL SKILLS

What am I learning?	I am learning to distinguish features of a sentence (e.g., first word, capitalization, ending punctuation).
Why am I learning this?	So that I can write better sentences.
How will I know that I have learned it?	When I can find the first word in a sentence. When I can find the capitalized letter to start the sentence. When I can find the ending punctuation.

SOCIAL STUDIES: EXPLORATIONS OF THE AMERICAS

What am I learning?	I am learning to locate land claimed by Spain, France, England, Portugal, the Netherlands, Sweden, and Russia.
Why am I learning this?	So that I understand the development of the Americas after European contact and conquest.
How will I know that I have learned it?	When I can name the location claimed by each country (Spain, France, England, Portugal, the Netherlands, Sweden, and Russia).

Return to Module 1. Starting on page 17, we devoted time to laying the foundation for generating success criteria beyond content learning intentions. With that in mind, what are the causes of and potential solutions to exclusively procedural success criteria? How would you edit these success criteria to incorporate additional learning intentions?

CHALLENGE 3: PRODUCT-FOCUSED

Learning is a process and there are important milestones throughout the process that give us insight into how our learners are progressing in their learning. Far too often, success criteria focus on the final product and inadvertently minimize the process necessary to arrive at that product.

> Far too often, success criteria focus on the final product and inadvertently minimize the process necessary to arrive at that product.

In mathematics, we often jump straight to correctly solving a computation problem. In history and English language arts, the inclination is to focus on essays, tests, and projects. In science, an example of product-focused success criteria is "I can create a model of cellular reproduction and use it to explain the process." What milestones or indicators exist along this learning journey that allow learners to monitor their progress and teachers to check for understanding? If a linear progression is not appropriate (e.g., proofs in geometry, human impact on the environment, multigenre writing, learning about different forms of government), what collective evidence will provide a more comprehensive picture of success? This is an important point. Students can use well-constructed success criteria to monitor their own progress toward the expected learning or collective indicators. Furthermore, are there social-emotional and language learning intentions that should inform the success criteria? Success criteria should not be limited to the end goal.

Module 2: What Are the Challenges to Creating and Implementing Success Criteria?

37

ELEMENTARY MATHEMATICS: COMPUTATION

What am I learning?	I am learning about subtracting numbers.
Why am I learning this?	So that I can subtract 10 and 100.
How will I know that I have learned it?	When I can correctly solve 15 subtraction problems.

ELEMENTARY ENGLISH LANGUAGE ARTS: WRITING

What am I learning?	I am learning to introduce a topic and state my opinion.
Why am I learning this?	So that I can tell people my opinion.
How will I know that I have learned it?	When I can include all items on the writing checklist.

MIDDLE SCHOOL SCIENCE: CONSERVATION OF MATTER

What am I learning?	I am learning about chemical reactions.
Why am I learning this?	So that I can understand how atoms stay the same but rearrange to form new molecules or compounds.
How will I know that I have learned it?	When I can balance simple chemical equations using subscripts and coefficients.

HIGH SCHOOL SOCIAL STUDIES: ECONOMICS

What am I learning?	I am learning about competition among buyers and sellers.
Why am I learning this?	So that I understand a market price.
How will I know that I have learned it?	When I can predict prices based on information about buyers and sellers.

When you looked at these non-examples, you likely perceived a lack of clarity in what was going on in each scenario. For example, the computation in elementary mathematics statements leaves us asking what kind of subtraction problems are meant. The *why* statement literally suggests that learners will solve one problem, 100 − 10, when this teacher likely means subtracting multiples of 10 from a given number or subtracting 10 or 100 from a wide range of values. This isn't clear as written due to a singular focus on the end product. That is exactly our point. What causes us to focus on the product and ignore the process? How do we avoid this challenge? Add your and your colleagues' thoughts to the box that follows.

CHALLENGE 4: NOT MEASURABLE

Another challenge that contributes to the disconnect in our learners' understanding of expectations is the measurability of success criteria. For example, success criteria that add a qualifier, or refer to a highly abstract concept or idea, are often not measurable by us or our students. This creates a situation where both the teacher and the learners are not only unclear about what success looks like, but they will find it very difficult to translate the success criteria into actionable steps toward the learning intention. As we will see in an upcoming module, success criteria that are not measurable can impede the opportunities to engage in deliberate practice, meta-cognition, and the giving and receiving of feedback. Consider the following nonmeasurable success criteria.

HIGH SCHOOL GEOMETRY: REASONING, LINES, AND TRANSFORMATION

What am I learning?	I am learning about the relationships between angles formed by two lines intersected by a transversal.
Why am I learning this?	So that I can prove the two lines are parallel.
How will I know that I have learned it?	When I can reason quantitatively. When I can engage in critical thinking. When I can know if two lines are parallel.

ELEMENTARY SCIENCE: WEATHER

What am I learning?	I am learning that the analysis of weather data is used to predict weather events.
Why am I learning this?	So that I can better understand how weather events impact ecosystems.
How will I know that I have learned it?	When I can thoroughly analyze weather data. When I can make the best weather predictions for a given area.

ELEMENTARY ENGLISH LANGUAGE ARTS: SPEAKING AND LISTENING

What am I learning?	I am learning to describe people, places, things, and events.
Why am I learning this?	So that people want to listen to me.
How will I know that I have learned it?	When I can express my ideas. When I can use relevant details.

ELEMENTARY SOCIAL STUDIES: EVERYDAY LIFE ACROSS TIME

What am I learning?	I am learning about transportation methods from the past.
Why am I learning this?	So that I understand how people went places.
How will I know that I have learned it?	When I can explain how transportation works.

How would we make these success criteria more measurable? What do you see as the causes of this particular challenge?

CHALLENGE 5: AGENDA OR SET OF DIRECTIONS

Oftentimes our attempts to provide as much clarity as possible move our success criteria away from learning and toward an agenda or set of instructions. For example, in mathematics, we may provide instructions for how to solve a problem instead of focusing on the content, practices, and dispositions associated with the learning of a particular topic. In science, we can easily turn the learning intention for a laboratory investigation or experiment into an agenda or list of instructions about what to do before, during, and after the experiment. In reading and writing, we focus on rules or procedures. In history and social studies, we focus on the chronological order of tasks to be completed.

> Oftentimes our attempts to provide as much clarity as possible move our success criteria away from learning and toward an agenda or set of instructions.

ELEMENTARY MATHEMATICS: NUMBER LINES

What am I learning?	I am learning about number lines.
Why am I learning this?	So that I can use them to solve problems.
How will I know that I have learned it?	When I can draw a straight line. When I can mark off the number line. When I can label the number line.

HIGH SCHOOL PHYSICS: ONE-DIMENSIONAL MOTION

What am I learning?	I am learning about motion in one dimension.
Why am I learning this?	So that I can solve kinematics equations.
How will I know that I have learned it?	When I can read the problem. When I can draw a diagram of the problem. When I can list the known variables. When I can identify what I am solving for. When I can select the right equation. When I can solve for the unknown variable.

HIGH SCHOOL ENGLISH LANGUAGE ARTS: LITERATURE

What am I learning?	I am learning to determine the meaning of words and phrases using word parts.
Why am I learning this?	So that I can figure out words as I am reading.
How will I know that I have learned it?	When I can identify prefixes. When I can identify suffixes. When I can identify roots or bases.

ELEMENTARY SOCIAL STUDIES: PHYSICAL AND HUMAN GEOGRAPHY

What am I learning?	I am learning about geographical features.
Why am I learning this?	So that I can describe our local region.
How will I know that I have learned it?	When I can name the characteristics of deserts. When I can name the characteristics of mountains. When I can name the characteristics of coastal areas.

How would we make these success criteria more about learning and less like an agenda or set of directions? What do you see as the causes of this particular challenge?

SUCCESS CRITERIA SELF-ASSESSMENT

Let's apply the list of challenges created by you and your colleagues on page 33 and the five challenges just described to help us self-monitor, self-reflect, and self-evaluate how we create and implement success criteria. Locate and record previous, current, or future learning intentions and success criteria in the space provided. Then, with your colleagues, discuss and analyze each example. Do you recognize any of the five challenges in your success criteria? Does this provide insight into the data collected in the Introduction (page 4) when you posed the following question to your students: *How will you know that you have learned the information or met the day's success criteria?* Here are some additional reflective questions to guide your discussion and analysis, which are also included in the Introduction.

- Do my success criteria truly represent the learning intentions for my learners?

- Did I pick the best option for implementing success criteria based on the type of learning expected of my students?

- Am I using success criteria to support my students taking ownership of their learning?

PREVIOUS, CURRENT, OR FUTURE LEARNING INTENTIONS AND SUCCESS CRITERIA	MY THOUGHTS ABOUT AND RESPONSES TO THE REFLECTIVE QUESTIONS ABOUT SUCCESS CRITERIA	MY COLLEAGUES' THOUGHTS AND RESPONSES	NEXT STEPS IN MY OWN LEARNING ABOUT SUCCESS CRITERIA

OVERCOMING CHALLENGES

Success criteria are more than *I can* statements. Each of the challenges described is brought about by the insistence that these teachers only use *I can* statements to answer the question: *How will I know that I have learned it?* Although *I can* statements are one option, and in many instances a great option, they are not the only approach and do not communicate success criteria effectively in all instances. This narrow view of success criteria leads to circular phrasing, too much emphasis on procedural learning, a hyperfocus on a product, criteria that are not measurable, and/or agenda items and a set of directions. Then, learners struggle with knowing what success looks like for a given intention. In a remote learning environment, these challenges are exacerbated by the fact that we are more than an arm's length away from learners. Thus,

clarity around what success looks like for both us and our learners is paramount. If our view of how to articulate success is solely focused on *I can* statements, we miss opportunities to provide expectations in collective learning, concept attainment, guided inquiry, project-based learning, and problem-solving teaching.

Returning to the concept of a playbook, we will devote entire modules to other ways of communicating what success looks like in our schools and classrooms.

> If our view of how to articulate success is solely focused on *I can* statements, we miss opportunities to provide expectations in collective learning, concept attainment, guided inquiry, project-based learning, and problem-solving teaching.

Ways of communicating criteria for success:

- *I can* statements
- *We can* statements
- Single-point rubrics
- Analytic/holistic rubrics
- Teacher modeling
- Exemplars
- Co-constructing criteria for success

We want to emphasize that there is no one best option. Some options work better than others, depending on the lesson. The determining factors about which of the above options to use once again take us back to the three reflective questions. If you and your colleagues need to refresh your memory, turn back to page 7 or page 41. To ensure we encode these three questions, retrieve them from your memory and write them in the space provided.

Again, *I can* statements are one way to share expectations of success with learners; however, in each of the previous examples, the sole use of an *I can* statement may impede learners as they engage in the acquisition of complex concepts and then apply those concepts and thinking to other contexts (transfer). This, in turn, becomes an equity issue—the topic of our next module.

Now that you have finished this module, rate yourself on each of the following success criteria using the four-item scale. Use the space provided at the end to self-reflect on your own learning. What will you do next with this information? You may not yet be at the expert level, as it takes time to integrate knowledge into practice.

- I can describe challenges associated with creating and implementing success criteria.

  Novice > Apprentice > Practitioner > Expert

- I can explain ways to overcome common challenges associated with creating and implementing success criteria.

  Novice > Apprentice > Practitioner > Expert

- I can list different ways of implementing success criteria.

  Novice > Apprentice > Practitioner > Expert

- I can work with my peers to analyze success criteria.

  Novice > Apprentice > Practitioner > Expert

NOTES

_____
_____
_____
_____
_____
_____
_____
_____
_____
_____
_____
_____
_____
_____
_____
_____
_____
_____
_____
_____
_____
_____
_____
_____
_____
_____

MODULE 3
HOW DO SUCCESS CRITERIA PAVE THE WAY FOR EQUITY?

Before you engage with the information in this module, rate yourself on each of the following success criteria using the four-item scale:

- I can describe what I mean by equity of access and opportunity for learning.

- I can explain how high-impact, high-quality success criteria pave the way for equity.

- I can compare and contrast different ways of implementing success criteria.

- I can work with my peers to analyze success criteria for equity of access and opportunity.

High-impact, high-quality success criteria pave the way for equity. But before we move on, let's devote some time to developing a definition of equity.

YOUR TURN!

Using any resources available to you, locate two or three different definitions of equity. Write them in the space provided. Then circle the words that stand out to you. Explain why these words stand out to you. Add this self-reflection in the space provided.

Merriam-Webster provides multiple definitions for the word *equity*. However, the first definition listed states that equity is "a justice according to natural law or right" (Merriam-Webster, 2020a). Take a moment to circle the word "right" in our definition. This begs the question: the right to what? We believe that equity in education asserts that each student has the right to a high-quality education. As a result, each student should be given equity of access and opportunity to the highest level of learning. This equity of access and opportunity is actualized when learners are offered the following:

- Multiple means of representing their content, practices, and dispositions
- Multiple ways of expressing their learning
- Multiple forms of engaging in the learning (CAST, 2018)

These three features of what has come to be known as Universal Design for Learning create a learning environment that values each individual learner and their unique identify profile. By offering multiple means of representing learning, expressing learning, and engaging in learning, we stand a greater chance of ensuring *all* learners will have access and opportunity to the highest level of learning.

YOUR TURN!

Pause for a moment to reflect on your own school or classroom. In the space provided, list how you offer the following:

> MULTIPLE MEANS OF REPRESENTING THEIR CONTENT, PRACTICES, AND DISPOSITIONS

> MULTIPLE WAYS OF EXPRESSING THEIR LEARNING

> MULTIPLE FORMS OF ENGAGING IN THE LEARNING

Our goal over the next several modules is to purposefully, intentionally, and deliberately create and implement success criteria that lead to learners participating in multiple forms of representing, expressing, and engaging in learning.

The starting point for equity lies in our expectations and beliefs about our students and their learning. These expectations manifest themselves in our success criteria. If we have high expectations for our learners, we often articulate these expectations through high-quality success criteria.

> The starting point for equity lies in our expectations and beliefs about our students and their learning.

Let's return to the social studies success criteria presented in Module 2. As you recall, these success criteria were highlighted because of the challenges they evoked in their implementation. However, look closer at the specific phrasing of these criteria and another trend emerges.

ANCIENT EGYPT
I can locate rivers and describe how they supported permanent settlement and civilizations.

EXPLORATIONS OF THE AMERICAS
I can name the location claimed by each country (Spain, France, England, Portugal, the Netherlands, Sweden, and Russia).

ECONOMICS
I can predict prices based on information about buyers and sellers.

EVERYDAY LIFE ACROSS TIME
I can explain how transportation works.

PHYSICAL AND HUMAN GEOGRAPHY
I can name the characteristics of deserts.

I can name the characteristics of mountains.

I can name the characteristics of coastal areas.

These *I can* statements represent low-level cognitive expectations that reflect a narrow view of what successful learning in social studies looks like. After all, we have yet to find a social studies teacher who hopes that in 20 years their learners will remember the characteristics of coastal areas.

How we create and implement success criteria communicates our expectations and beliefs about what our students can know, understand, and be able to do. A narrow reductionist approach to success sends the message that our learners are seen as fact-regurgitators and standardized test-takers. A narrow reductionist approach to success excludes those learners who might need a different access point or another opportunity to show you what they know. A narrow reductionist approach to success treats the learner as a one-size-fits-all student. By widening our perspective about what success looks like, taking into account the individual profiles of our learners, we communicate to our learners that success criteria allow us to incorporate different points for accessing, processing, and then demonstrating learning. By creating and implementing success criteria that expect and offer multiple means of representing learning, expressing learning, and engaging in learning, we stand a greater chance of engaging *all* learners, providing equity of access and opportunity to the highest level of learning.

> By creating and implementing success criteria that expect and offer multiple means of representing learning, expressing learning, and engaging in learning, we stand a greater chance of engaging *all* learners, providing equity of access and opportunity to the highest level of learning.

YOUR TURN!

In the space provided and in your own words, summarize how high-quality success criteria pave the way for equity. Keep this summary close by. We will revisit equity throughout the playbook and then in Module 14.

DIFFERENT WAYS OF IMPLEMENTING SUCCESS CRITERIA

As we have said repeatedly, there is no one right way to define the targeted learning outcome. There are at least seven different ways of knowing and showing success criteria, and these seven are the focus of this playbook:

1. *I Can* **Statements:** This form of success criteria is the most popular, but may not always be the most effective means of implementation. *I can* statements are explicit and direct statements about what individual learners must do to demonstrate their learning. These statements also guide us in what to look for from individual learners.

2. *We Can* **Statements:** These explicit and direct statements take a collaborative view of learning. Rather than what individual learners must do, this form of success criteria highlights the value of collective learning and what learners and teachers are expected to do, together.

3. **Single-Point Rubrics:** Rather than different levels of quality, a single-point rubric provides the expectations for mastery in a process, task, or product. In other words, only a single level of quality is provided for each expectation.

4. **Analytic/Holistic Rubrics:** Rubrics provide learners with the expectations for the process, task, or product along with descriptions of the level of quality for each expectation.

5. **Teacher Modeling:** Helping learners understand expectations of success can come from us modeling the *content*, *practices*, and *dispositions*. This modeling allows learners to see success in action. Learners use the model to guide their own work toward the learning intention.

6. **Exemplars:** We can provide worked examples and/or exemplars of processes or finished tasks or products. Worked examples provide a comparison for learners to use in their own work, while exemplars possess all the expectations for success and can truly be a model for their learning path.

7. **Co-constructing Criteria for Success:** The final way to implement success criteria is by co-constructing those expectations with learners. The process of co-constructing is a collaborative effort between teachers and students as they set the criteria for success before engaging in the work.

Before we conclude this module, take a moment to compare and contrast these seven approaches to implementing criteria for success. How do you see them as similar? How do you see them as different? What are your thoughts on these different approaches?

YOUR TURN!

Select one of the non-examples in Module 2. For instance, you could select "English Language Arts: Foundational Skills." Here is that specific non-example:

What am I learning?	I am learning to distinguish features of a sentence (e.g., first word, capitalization, ending punctuation).
Why am I learning this?	So that I can write better sentences.
How will I know I that have learned it?	When I can find the first word in a sentence. When I can find the capitalized letter to start the sentence. When I can find the ending punctuation.

Once you have flipped back to Module 2 and selected one of the non-examples, analyze the creation and implementation of the success criteria with your colleagues. Use the following questions to guide your discussion:

1. Do the success criteria offer multiple ways for learners to represent their learning?

2. Do the success criteria offer multiple ways for learners to express their learning?

3. Do the success criteria offer multiple ways of engaging in the learning?

Use the space provided to record the highlights of your conversation. Also, how might you revise one of these non-examples to offer multiple means of representing learning, expressing learning, and engaging all learners to ensure equity of access and opportunity to achieve the highest level of learning?

From this point forward, we will use this reflective module to ensure that our focus on success criteria paves the way for equity of access and opportunity for all learners to the highest level of learning.

Now that you have finished this module, rate yourself on each of the following success criteria using the four-item scale. Use the space provided at the end to self-reflect on your own learning. What will you do next with this information? You may not yet be at the expert level, as it takes time to integrate knowledge into practice.

- I can describe what I mean by equity of access and opportunity for learning.

| Novice | Apprentice | Practitioner | Expert |

- I can explain how high-impact, high-quality success criteria pave the way for equity.

| Novice | Apprentice | Practitioner | Expert |

- I can compare and contrast different ways of implementing success criteria.

| Novice | Apprentice | Practitioner | Expert |

- I can work with my peers to analyze success criteria for equity of access and opportunity.

| Novice | Apprentice | Practitioner | Expert |

NOTES

_____

_____

_____

_____

_____

_____

_____

_____

_____

_____

_____

_____

_____

_____

_____

_____

_____

_____

_____

_____

_____

_____

_____

_____

PART 2

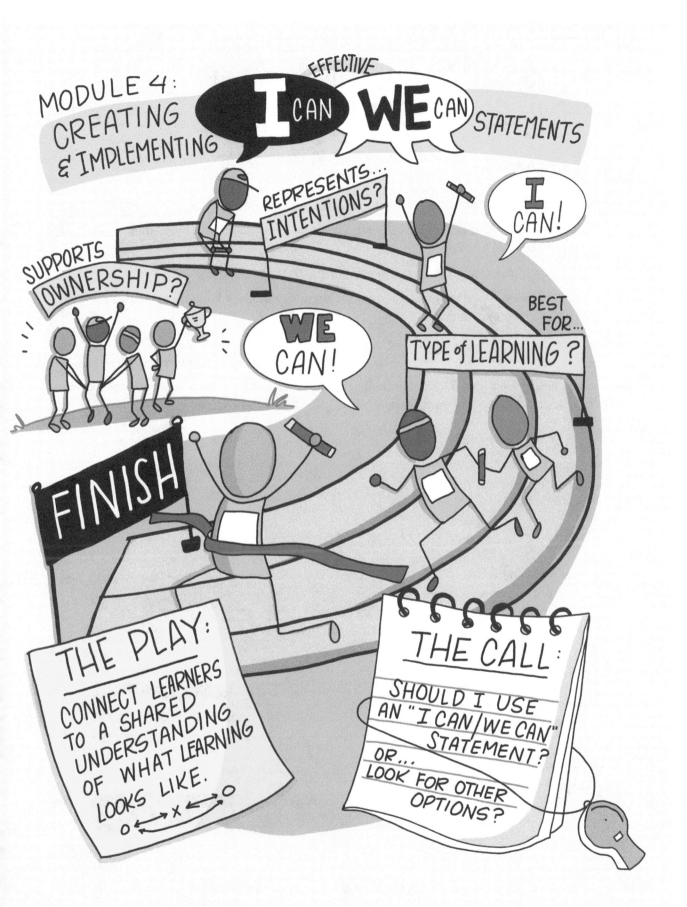

MODULE 4
CREATING AND IMPLEMENTING EFFECTIVE *I CAN/WE CAN* STATEMENTS

I can and *We can* statements allow learners to do the following:

- See the specific actions they must do *today* to demonstrate learning.
- Map out the progression of the learning experience toward the learning intention—the flow of the day's learning.
- Focus their attention on the most relevant aspects of the day's learning.
- Identify the *evidence* they must produce to demonstrate their learning at various points in the learning experience.

Before you engage with the information in this module, rate yourself on each of the following success criteria using the four-item scale:

- I can describe the critical components of *I can* statements.

| Novice | Apprentice | Practitioner | Expert |

- I can explain the differences between *I can* and *We can* statements.

| Novice | Apprentice | Practitioner | Expert |

- I can develop *I can* and *We can* statements of increasing complexity.

| Novice | Apprentice | Practitioner | Expert |

- I can distinguish when to use *I can* statements versus other tools for success criteria.

| Novice | Apprentice | Practitioner | Expert |

I can statements are quite likely the most well-known and commonly used approach to creating and sharing criteria for success. Written from the learner's perspective, these direct and explicit statements articulate what learners are expected to do in order to demonstrate their learning. These statements are phrased in a way that forecasts a positive future. In doing so, they are aspirational and allow students to allocate resources (time, thinking, help-seeking) to obtaining the goal. As strange as this sounds, these statements are a form of "thought control," or cognitive restructuring; they encourage students to persevere in their learning and maintain a mindset that they will eventually attain success. Feltz and colleagues (2008) noted the value of these types of statements as builders of efficacy in athletes as they considered aspects of their sports that they wanted to perfect.

In addition to *I can* statements, there are times when we strive to leverage the learner's individual strengths toward a collective learning experience.

In this situation, we can easily communicate the expectations of collective learning by phrasing these statements as *We can*. Drawing from the verbs within a particular standard, *I can* and *We can* success criteria statements should do the following:

- Be actionable.
- Focus on learning, not the task.
- Provide the necessary components for meeting the intent of the learning.
- Appear in student-friendly language.
- Often include more than one statement per learning intention.
- Incorporate content, practices, and dispositions.

YOUR TURN!

Take a look at the following examples and non-examples. In the last column, identify which of the characteristics of high-quality success criteria are missing from the non-examples. The first one is done for you.

LEARNING INTENTIONS	EXAMPLES OF SUCCESS CRITERIA	NON-EXAMPLES OF SUCCESS CRITERIA	WHAT'S WRONG WITH THE NON-EXAMPLE?
Mathematics			
We are learning to select fluent subtraction strategies.	• We can select an efficient and appropriate subtraction strategy based on the numbers and situation. • We can defend our reasoning to our peers and understand their reasoning too. • We can apply the strategy to find an accurate solution.	• I can do my best to persist through two-step subtraction problems.	• *Do my best* is not actionable • Does not provide the necessary components for showing success

CONTINUED

LEARNING INTENTIONS	EXAMPLES OF SUCCESS CRITERIA	NON-EXAMPLES OF SUCCESS CRITERIA	WHAT'S WRONG WITH THE NON-EXAMPLE?
We are learning to estimate length measurements.	• We can estimate length using our personal benchmarks for centimeters, meters, and kilometers. • We can estimate length using a visual referent for comparison. • We can describe our estimate using mathematical language: *about, close to, more than, less than, between*. • We can evaluate the reasonableness of a peer's solution based on our estimate.	• Students will give accurate estimates for a variety of lengths.	
I am learning about the role of irrational numbers within the number system.	• I can explain the difference between a rational and an irrational number. • I can collaborate to name irrational numbers and estimate their approximate locations on a number line using rational numbers as benchmarks.	• I know what an irrational number is. • I know how to convert $0.\overline{66}$ into a rational number. • I know the decimal expansion of $\sqrt{2}$ is approximately 1.41.	
Science			
I am learning about the law of conservation of mass in isolated systems.	• I can balance a simple chemical reaction. • I can balance a complex reaction. • I can predict the products of a chemical reaction.	• I can complete an exit ticket on chemical reactions with 80% accuracy.	
We are learning about the role of energy transfer in the rock cycle.	• We can identify each of the three types of rocks. • We can describe how their properties provide evidence of how they were formed.	• Students will demonstrate success by correctly answering questions while modeling the rock cycle.	

LEARNING INTENTIONS	EXAMPLES OF SUCCESS CRITERIA	NON-EXAMPLES OF SUCCESS CRITERIA	WHAT'S WRONG WITH THE NON-EXAMPLE?
I am learning about the impact of humans on the environment.	• I can give examples of how humans impact the environment. • I can describe how these actions impact specific parts of the ecosystem. • I can collaboratively propose possible solutions that will lessen that impact.	• I can give examples of how humans impact the environment, describe how they impact the environment, and propose solutions.	
I am learning about energy transfer in matter.	• I can describe how matter changes from one form to another.	• The student will understand the relationship between the flow of energy and the states of matter.	
English Language Arts			
I am learning to analyze the impact of word choice on tone.	• I can describe the difference between mood and tone. • I can identify words that might set the tone. • I can analyze the words and identify the tone.	• I can analyze the impact of word choice on tone.	
I am learning about informational text structures.	• I can use signal words to identify the structure of a text. • I can explain the characteristics of common types of text structures. • I can use my knowledge about text structures to organize my notes.	• I can write using informational text structures. • I can name five text structures.	
Social Studies			
We are learning about the contributions of Muslim scholars and their impact on later civilizations.	• We can describe contributions from Muslim scholars in the areas of science and medicine. • We can describe contributions from Muslim scholars in the areas of philosophy, art, and literature. • We can describe contributions from Muslim scholars in the area of mathematics.	• I can explain the significance of the Qur'an. • I can recall information from the video about Muslim scholars.	

HOW DO WE GENERATE *I CAN* AND *WE CAN* STATEMENTS?

Now we turn our attention to how we develop *I can* or *We can* statements. These statements come from the deconstruction of the learning intention. In other words, what are the necessary components or steps that lead to the learning intention? Return to the image of the target in Module 1 (see Figure 1.1 on page 17). Notice that each success criterion moves learners closer to the bull's-eye or targeted learning intention. As we pointed out earlier, there are often multiple success criteria for each learning intention. This is how we should generate success criteria. Consider the following examples.

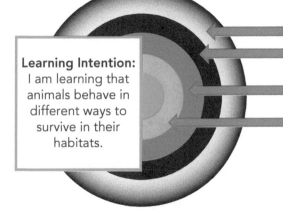

Learning Intention: We are learning the many ways mathematicians make sense of and represent quotients and remainders.

Success Criterion 1: We can select a strategy and solve for a quotient and remainder.

Success Criterion 2: We can represent the quotient and the remainder using equations, rectangular arrays, or area models.

Success Criterion 3: We can explain the meaning of the quotient and the remainder within the representation and the problem context.

Success Criterion 4: We can compare our reasoning to a peer's and analyze differences and similarities in our strategies and representations.

Learning Intention: I am learning that animals behave in different ways to survive in their habitats.

Success Criterion 1: I can list different animal behaviors.

Success Criterion 2: I can describe how animals gather food, find shelter, defend themselves, and rear their young.

Success Criterion 3: I can use evidence to infer how these behaviors help animals to survive.

Success Criterion 4: I can construct an explanation for why specific behaviors depend on specific habitats and environments.

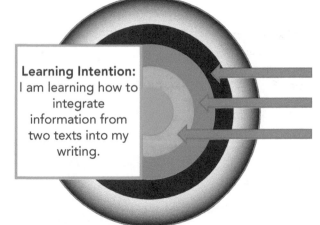

Learning Intention: I am learning how to integrate information from two texts into my writing.

Success Criterion 1: I can extract key details from texts.

Success Criterion 2: I can identify places of agreement and disagreement in the texts.

Success Criterion 3: I can use the information from my analysis in my writing.

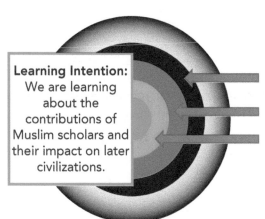

Learning Intention: We are learning about the contributions of Muslim scholars and their impact on later civilizations.

Success Criterion 1: We can describe contributions from Muslim scholars in the areas of science and medicine.
Success Criterion 2: We can describe contributions from Muslim scholars in the areas of philosophy, art, and literature.
Success Criterion 3: We can describe contributions from Muslim scholars in the area of mathematics.

In these examples, the success criteria not only move learners closer to the targeted learning intention, but they also move toward a higher level of complexity or greater depth of knowledge. In the math example, a similar progression from solving and representing to explaining and analyzing emerges as learners move closer to the target. In the science example, listing different animal behaviors requires a different level of thinking than constructing an explanation about specific behaviors in specific habitats. In the English language arts example, students move from identifying details to comparing those details to integrating them into their written responses. And in social studies, learners should progress from describing the contributions of Muslim scholars to analyzing and evaluating their impact on later civilizations.

When we deconstruct the learning intention to generate success criteria, we should develop a pathway for the learner that guides them toward the bull's-eye. This progression begins with a **foundational idea** (e.g., division problems can

> When we deconstruct the learning intention to generate success criteria, we should develop a pathway for the learner that guides them toward the bull's-eye.

have quotients and remainders, animals have behaviors, text structures, general contributions of Muslim scholars), then moves to **multiple ideas** (e.g., quotients and remainders can be represented in multiple ways, animals have specific behaviors, text structures provide information, Muslim scholars contributed to science and medicine). From there, the progression should move learners toward **relational thinking** and then **application of the concept and thinking** (e.g., construct an explanation, justify a strategy, use text structures to organize notes, evaluate or analyze the impact of Muslim scholars). Like hitting a target, you only get some of the "points" if you hit one of the outside circles. When you hit the bull's-eye, you get all of the "points"; in this case, you have met all of the success criteria.

GUIDED PRACTICE

For the following learning intentions, generate *I can* and/or *We can* statements that deconstruct the learning intention and create a learning progression (i.e., foundational idea, multiple components, relational thinking, and then application of the concept and thinking). After you and your colleagues have completed the guided practice, please turn to page 71 for suggested answers.

	HIGH SCHOOL MATHEMATICS	MIDDLE SCHOOL SCIENCE	MIDDLE SCHOOL ENGLISH LANGUAGE ARTS	ELEMENTARY SOCIAL STUDIES
What is the learning intention?	We are learning why multiple representations of the solutions for a system of equations help model the meaning of the solutions within a context.	I am learning about the role of energy transfer in the rock cycle.	I am learning about the ways in which a poem's form contributes to its meaning.	I am learning about the effects of the Gold Rush on settlements.
What are the success criteria? (*I can/We can* statements) • Foundational idea • Multiple ideas • Relational thinking • Application of the concept and thinking				

There is one final point we want to make here. We are often asked about the number of *I can* statements. There is no magic number! Instead, how many *I can* statements are needed to thoroughly define what success looks like for the learning intentions? That determines how many. There is always the next day.

YOUR TURN!

Return to the table in Module 1 on page 20 where you and your colleagues generated the list of what learners would say and do if they mastered the learning intention. Use the space provided to rewrite the learning intention and then create your progression of success criteria that will guide you and your learners toward the learning intention. Refer to the characteristics of high-quality *I can* or *We can* statements at the beginning of this module.

LEARNING INTENTIONS	I CAN/WE CAN STATEMENTS

Before moving on, take another look at your statements. Are there success criteria that are best met through collective learning? Where can you integrate collaboration through *We can*?

LIMITATIONS OF *I CAN* AND *WE CAN* STATEMENTS

We started with *I can/We can* statements because they are a common and powerful way to ensure that students understand what success looks like (when they are constructed well, that is). But there are times when these statements are not the most effective way to ensure that students understand what success looks like. For example, imagine a group of students writing an argumentative essay in science. They have taken a position and are tasked with supplying facts that support their claims. The risk with *I can* or *We can* statements in this example is that the writing may become formulaic. We don't want to limit writing to mechanics and conventions. And we don't want students' writing to sound the same as everyone else's writing. In this case, other options are probably more appropriate, as we will see in future modules. Remember to refer back to the reflective questions to help decide when to use *I can*, *We can*, or another option for creating and implementing success criteria.

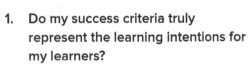

1. Do my success criteria truly represent the learning intentions for my learners?

2. Did I pick the best option for implementing success criteria based on the type of learning expected of my students?

3. Am I using success criteria to support my students taking ownership of their learning?

In addition, sometimes success is better modeled and demonstrated rather than described. In those cases, *I can* statements are of limited value and other options are likely to be more effective. Further, there are times when rubrics allow students to see a scale of success that is much more nuanced than *I can* statements. But when *I can* statements work, they work well. As fifth-grader Emelio says, "I can do a lot of things. More things now than before. I have accomplished all of these [pointing to a list of *I can* statements]. Do you want to see?"

Let's take another look at the **non-examples** for the success criteria beginning on page 61 in this module.

- The subtraction problem involved persistence, a very important disposition in mathematics learning. To better define the target here, we will need to offer more clarity about what is meant by persistence.

- The science non-examples involved answering questions and modeling. Although this non-example was focused on a task (not learning), asking questions and using models are both important science practices. What makes this a non-example is that there is not a clear indication about what was involved in the modeling. In other words, persisting, questioning, and modeling

are important aspects of mathematics and science learning. They are just not best represented here by high-quality success criteria.

- The English language arts non-example focuses on recall rather than the striving set expectations that learners would engage in in rich text-based experiences. These expectations or success criteria should guide learners to use text evidence in the analysis of what they read.

- The social studies non-example had success criteria focused on specific activities. This bypasses the relevancy of their learning and squelches the learners' understanding of the contributions of Muslim scholars to the global context beyond just a single video.

You may have encountered similar situations when creating your own *I can* or *We can* statements. If the statements become more focused on a product or disposition—or they simply need further explanation about what success looks like—consider other approaches to make the expectations clear. This leads us into the next module and a second approach for creating and implementing success criteria.

PATHWAY TO EQUITY: HOW DO WE GET ALL LEARNERS TO ENGAGE WITH *I CAN/WE CAN* STATEMENTS?

Just because we have created *I can* or *We can* statements and posted them on the board does not guarantee that our learners will engage with them and know what success looks like for the day's learning. There are several approaches for ensuring that learners understand and can use the *I can* statements.

1. *Explicitly share them at the start of the learning experience.* This can be done by having learners discuss the *I can* statements with their peers and share

the thoughts, questions, or ideas that come to mind when they see or hear the day's statements. This can be done using a think-pair-share or breakout rooms during remote learning.

2. *Provide them in interactive notebooks.* We can ask learners to write or record the statements in their interactive online notebooks (e.g., Jamboard, Google Docs) for referencing throughout the learning experience. When learners are working in their interactive notebooks, they can then link specific pages in their notebooks to specific *I can* statements.

3. *Return to them during the lesson and use them as checks for understanding.* As we move through the learning experience, we can ask our learners which *I can* statement we are working on and where

we are going next. We can ask learners to demonstrate they "can" through a quick formative check for understanding. In cooperative learning groups or breakout rooms, learners can collectively provide evidence that "We can." This uses the statements to guide us through the learning.

4. *Use them at the end of the day as an exit ticket.* We can return to the *I can* or *We can* statements and use them for individual or collective reflection and closure. When these statements are used in an exit ticket or survey, we can see if learners are truly able to demonstrate the actions described in the statement. This provides valuable information about where to start tomorrow.

YOUR TURN!

As we close out this module, take a moment to map out how you will get your learners to engage in *I can* or *We can* statements within your classroom or remote learning environment. Be sure to add your own ideas to our list.

Now that you have finished this module, rate yourself on each of the following success criteria using the four-item scale. Use the space provided at the end to self-reflect on your own learning. What will you do next with this information? You may not yet be at the expert level, as it takes time to integrate knowledge into practice. Use this information to identify areas of continued learning.

- I can describe the critical components of *I can* statements.

- I can explain the differences between *I can* and *We can* statements.

- I can develop *I can* and *We can* statements of increasing complexity.

- I can distinguish when to use *I can* statements versus other tools for success criteria.

SUGGESTED ANSWERS FOR MODULE 4

	HIGH SCHOOL MATHEMATICS	MIDDLE SCHOOL SCIENCE	ENGLISH LANGUAGE ARTS	SOCIAL STUDIES
What is the learning intention?	We are learning why multiple representations of the solutions for a system of equations help model the meaning of the solutions within a context.	I am learning about the role of energy transfer in the rock cycle.	I am learning about the ways in which a poem's form contributes to its meaning.	I am learning about the effects of the Gold Rush on settlements.
What are the success criteria? (*I can/We can* statements) • Foundational idea • Multiple ideas • Relational thinking • Application of the concept and thinking	• I can solve a system of two equations approximately and explain the reasonableness of the approximate graphical solutions. (*foundational idea*) • I can solve a system of two equations and explain the relationship between the approximate graphical and exact algebraic solutions. (*multiple ideas*) • I can represent and solve a system of equations using multiple representations and explain the relationships among them. (*relational thinking*) • I can apply multiple, related mathematical models to make sense of the graphical and algebraic solutions for a system of equations within the context. (*application of the concept and thinking*)	• I can list the parts of the rock cycle. (*foundational idea*) • I can describe the processes that change rocks from one time to another. (*multiple ideas*) • I can explain the role of energy transfer in the rock cycle. (*relational thinking*) • We can analyze data to develop a model that shows the processes, rocks, and materials involved in the rock cycle. (*application of the concept and thinking*)	• I can identify the forms that a poet uses. (*foundational idea*) • I can describe the length of lines and their rhythms and how they contribute to meaning. (*multiple idea*) • I can compare poems and their use of various forms. (*relational thinking*) • I can write three poems using different forms to convey my intended meaning.	• I can identify where the Gold Rush occurred. • I can describe the reasons that people left home to find gold. • I can explain the difference between what people expected and what they experienced in the Gold Rush settlements. • I can describe the various roles of people who lived in the Gold Rush settlements.

NOTES

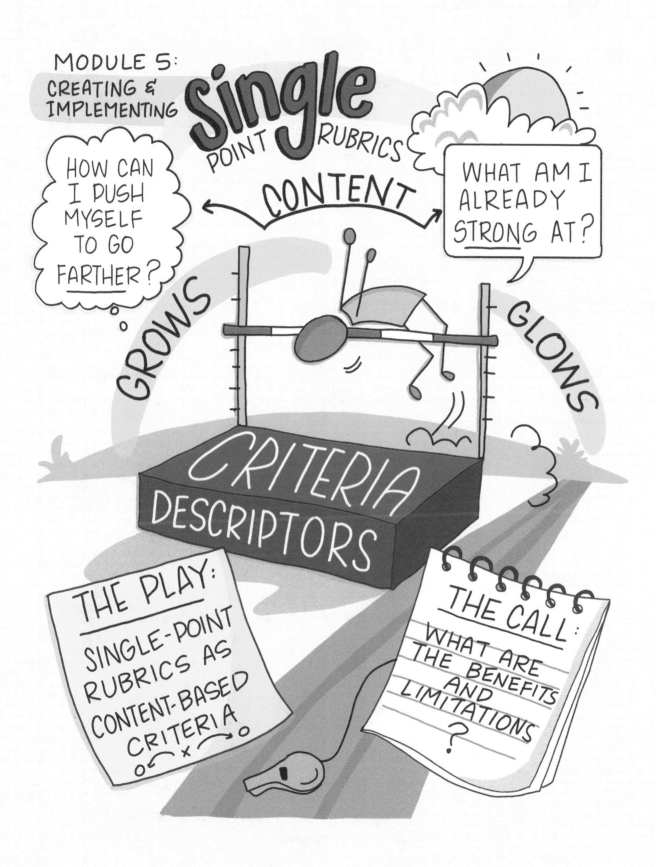

MODULE 5
CREATING AND IMPLEMENTING
SINGLE-POINT RUBRICS

Single-point rubrics allow learners to do the following:

- Work on different criteria at different times than their peers.
- Identify areas of growth and areas for improvement.
- Reflect on strengths and weaknesses.
- Be unrestrained by perceived boundaries (e.g., levels of success).
- Focus on expectations and not a score or rank.
- Demonstrate their mastery in different ways.
- Receive instructional scaffolding as they develop critical thinking skills.

Before you engage with the information in this module, rate yourself on each of the following success criteria using the four-item scale:

- I can describe a single-point rubric.

- I can explain when a single-point rubric is useful as a tool for success.

- I can create single-point rubrics aligned to the learning intentions.

- I can use single-point rubrics to organize feedback from peers and from teachers.

How do we create and share success criteria when learners will be working on different content at different times than their peers? What about practices and dispositions? What if students are learning remotely in an asynchronous environment? In a single learning experience or over the course of a unit, learners may find themselves engaged in processes, tasks, and products that differ from their peers or are occurring at different times than their peers. If learners are engaged in inquiry or problem-solving, there is no guarantee that they will all develop the same question or identify the same problem. If we are using centers or stations, each area will have different criteria for success.

Likewise, there are practices that transcend grade levels and standards. For example, the Common Core State Standards for Mathematical Practices and the Science and Engineering Practices have additional components within each specific practice (e.g., construction of viable arguments or engaging in argument from evidence) (National Governors Association Center for Best Practices & Council of Chief State School Officers, 2010; National Research Council, 2013). And learners may be working on different components of those practices at different times. Developing success criteria in these situations can be unmanageable if we focus solely on *I can* statements. One option is to create and share single-point rubrics.

1. Do my success criteria truly represent the learning intentions for my learners?

2. Did I pick the best option for implementing success criteria based on the type of learning expected of my students?

3. Am I using success criteria to support my students taking ownership of their learning?

Single-point rubrics provide a set of success criteria with a focus on one level of success: mastery. That is, the criteria do not have different levels of success as they do in analytic and holistic rubrics, and learners are focused on meeting only one level of success from a given set of success criteria. Students can utilize single-point rubrics to think critically about their learning progress, making note of the criteria that they have mastered and those that they are still working on. This level of focus makes single-point rubrics powerful in supporting learners in demonstrating their understanding through self-knowledge and self-assessment.

Single-point rubrics provide a set of success criteria with a focus on one level of success: mastery.

CONTENT-BASED CRITERIA WITHIN A SINGLE-POINT RUBRIC

In the following mathematics and English language arts examples, we provide content-based criteria within a single-point rubric.

GROWS	CRITERIA AND DESCRIPTORS	GLOWS
How I Can Strengthen My Work	For Learning About Subtraction	Strong Aspects of My Work
	I can use mental math to subtract 10 and 100.	
	I can use an open number line to take away.	
	I can use an open number line to find the difference between.	
	I can think addition to subtract.	
	I can use compensation to subtract.	
	I can select and defend a strategy of my choice to subtract three-digit numbers.	

GROWS	CRITERIA AND DESCRIPTORS	GLOWS
How I Can Strengthen My Work	For an Essay About a Filmed Drama	Strong Aspects of My Work
	I can identify the play with the full title, playwright, director, producing organization, and date.	
	I can describe the performances of at least two actors with descriptive examples to illustrate my opinions about their performances.	
	I can identify a major dramatic question that is answered in the play.	
	I can describe the incident that introduces the main conflict in the play.	
	I can describe the moment when the protagonist commits to their goal.	
	I can identify the moment in the play when the major dramatic question is answered.	
	I can describe how all major characters are affected by the conflict.	

How about the disciplinary practices and dispositions? Let's look at a way to make the targets visible and define the expectations for constructing a viable mathematical argument and engaging in argumentation with compelling evidence through a single-point rubric.

GROWS	CRITERIA AND DESCRIPTORS	GLOWS
How I Can Strengthen My Work	For Constructing a Viable Mathematical Argument	Strong Aspects of My Work
	My stated assumptions are mathematically accurate.	
	My argument draws upon mathematical definitions and previously established results.	
	My conjectures build a logical progression.	
	I justify my conclusions, communicate them to others, and respond to arguments of others.	
	My argument involves the use of multiple representations (e.g., objects, actions, drawings, diagrams, labeled equations).	

GROWS	CRITERIA AND DESCRIPTORS	GLOWS
How I Can Strengthen My Work	For Argumentation With Compelling Evidence and Reasons	Strong Aspects of My Work
	I compare and critique two arguments on the same topic and analyze whether they emphasize similar or different evidence and/or interpretations of facts.	
	I respectfully provide critiques about my peer's explanations, procedures, models, and questions by citing relevant evidence and posing and responding to questions that elicit pertinent elaboration and detail.	
	I construct, use, and/or present oral and written arguments supported by empirical evidence and scientific reasoning to support or refute an explanation or a model for a phenomenon or a solution to a problem.	
	I make an oral or written argument that supports or refutes the advertised performance of a device, process, or system, based on empirical evidence concerning whether or not the technology meets relevant criteria and constraints.	

YOUR TURN!

What do you and your colleagues believe are the benefits of using single-point rubrics? Note some of those benefits in the space provided.

You can see in the previous examples that the criteria and descriptors are flexible enough for learners to find different ways to demonstrate each of them. In addition, single-point rubrics scaffold learners as they develop critical thinking skills, an important learning disposition for learners. By focusing on growth and improvement, we can support and encourage positive learning dispositions.

The high-quality criteria and descriptors for single-point rubrics must have the same characteristics as high-quality *I can* or *We can* statements. We used *I can* statements in the content-based single-point rubrics, but remember that high-quality success criteria have the same essential characteristics even if they are created and shared in a different form.

> The high-quality criteria and descriptors for single-point rubrics must have the same characteristics as high-quality *I can* or *We can* statements.

HOW DO WE GENERATE SINGLE-POINT RUBRICS?

Generating single-point rubrics includes elements of developing *I can* or *We can* statements. The first step is to deconstruct the learning intention. Similar to *I can* statements, we first have to identify the necessary components or steps that lead to the learning intention. Each success criterion moves toward a higher level of complexity as you move down the single-point rubric. Revisit page 65 in Module 4. This is the exact process we utilized in the earlier examples.

Unlike *I can* or *We can* statements, however, additional descriptors are necessary for single-point rubrics focused on practices and dispositions. To be effective, these rubrics must identify the descriptors for each criterion that represents mastery. Why mastery? Because, single-point rubrics set the expectation level at mastery. Again, the criteria and descriptors should be perfectly aligned with the learning intention and not incorporate irrelevant details (e.g., including the name and date on the paper, cleaning up the center when finished). If you have previously developed rubrics that identify several levels of success, you can use the mastery level as the starting place for your single-point rubric.

GUIDED PRACTICE

For the following learning intentions, develop a single-point rubric. When finished, please turn to page 89 for suggested answers.

MATHEMATICS

TOPIC: ELEMENTARY PLACE VALUE

LEARNING INTENTION: I AM LEARNING WAYS NUMBERS CAN BE DECOMPOSED AND COMPOSED INTO GROUPS OF HUNDREDS, TENS, AND ONES.

GROWS	CRITERIA AND DESCRIPTORS	GLOWS
How I Can Strengthen My Work	For Learning About Decomposing and Composing Numbers Into Groups of Hundreds, Tens, and Ones	Strong Aspects of My Work

TOPIC: PLANTS AND THEIR ENVIRONMENT

LEARNING INTENTION: I AM LEARNING ABOUT THE PARTS OF A PLANT AND HOW THEY HELP THE PLANT SURVIVE.

GROWS	CRITERIA AND DESCRIPTORS	GLOWS
How I Can Strengthen My Work	For Learning About the Parts of a Plant and How They Help the Plant Survive	Strong Aspects of My Work

CONTINUED

CONTINUED

TOPIC: SPEAKING AND LISTENING

LEARNING INTENTION: I AM LEARNING TO EVALUATE A SPEAKER'S POINT OF VIEW, REASONING, AND USE OF EVIDENCE.

GROWS	CRITERIA AND DESCRIPTORS	GLOWS
How I Can Strengthen My Work	For Learning to Evaluate a Speaker's Point of View, Reasoning, and Use of Evidence	Strong Aspects of My Work

TOPIC: WORLD HISTORY

LEARNING INTENTION: I AM LEARNING ABOUT ARTISTIC AND ARCHITECTURAL TRADITIONS IN MESO-AMERICAN AND ANDEAN CIVILIZATIONS.

GROWS	CRITERIA AND DESCRIPTORS	GLOWS
How I Can Strengthen My Work	For Learning About Artistic and Architectural Traditions in Meso-American and Andean Civilizations	Strong Aspects of My Work

YOUR TURN!

Select a learning intention that involves self-knowledge or must allow for learners to work on different criteria at different times than their peers. Use the following template to build a single-point rubric.

Single-Point Rubric Template

GROWS	CRITERIA AND DESCRIPTORS	GLOWS
How I Can Strengthen My Work	For _____	Strong Aspects of My Work

PATHWAY TO EQUITY: HOW DO WE GET ALL LEARNERS TO ENGAGE WITH SINGLE-POINT RUBRICS?

Single-point rubrics are, by their very nature, engaging. However, the level or depth of engagement may vary among learners—from approaching it as a checklist to get through to truly using the criteria and descriptors to critically think about their learning. Fostering learner engagement with single-point rubrics lays the foundation for learners to monitor their own progress and to engage in self-reflection and self-evaluation. Single-point rubrics can also be used to facilitate conversations between students as they discuss each other's work. We will devote more time to these meta-cognitive skills in Module 11. For now, the takeaway here is that single-point rubrics are a starting point for meta-cognition.

> Single-point rubrics are a starting point for meta-cognition.

YOUR TURN!

So, how will you engage your learners in rubrics and ensure they continue to use them in their work? Use the space provided to map out a plan for creating and implementing single-point rubrics in your classroom or through your remote learning platform. Be sure to add your own ideas to our list if you feel a strategy is missing or you have one that works for you but is not on our list.

- Review the rubric before releasing students to engage in the work.

CONTINUED

CONTINUED

- Develop a plan for the day using Grows and Glows. Learners might map out where they will spend additional time during the learning experience based on where they need additional learning time.

- Have learners present their Glows and Grows to peers before moving forward in their learning.

- Have learners compile evidence in their interactive notebooks and reference the page number in their notebooks in either the Glows or Grows column of the single-point rubric.

Now that you have finished this module, rate yourself on each of the following success criteria using the four-item scale. Use the space provided at the end to self-reflect on your own learning. What will you do next with this information? You may not yet be at the expert level, as it takes time to integrate knowledge into practice. Use this information to identify areas of continued learning.

- I can describe a single-point rubric.

  Novice > Apprentice > Practitioner > Expert

- I can explain when a single-point rubric is useful as a tool for success.

  Novice > Apprentice > Practitioner > Expert

- I can create single-point rubrics aligned to the learning intentions.

  Novice > Apprentice > Practitioner > Expert

- I can use single-point rubrics to organize feedback from peers and from teachers.

  Novice > Apprentice > Practitioner > Expert

SUGGESTED ANSWERS FOR MODULE 5

TOPIC: ELEMENTARY PLACE VALUE

LEARNING INTENTION: I AM LEARNING WAYS NUMBERS CAN BE DECOMPOSED AND COMPOSED INTO GROUPS OF HUNDREDS, TENS, AND ONES.

GROWS	CRITERIA AND DESCRIPTORS	GLOWS
How I Can Strengthen My Work	For Learning About Decomposing and Composing Numbers Into Groups of Hundreds, Tens, and Ones	Strong Aspects of My Work
	I can describe the values of the digits in a number using hundreds, tens, and/or ones.	
	I can decompose a number into an equivalent set of bundles or groups of hundreds, tens, and/or ones.	
	I can compose bundles or groups of hundreds, tens, and/or ones to create an equivalent three-digit number.	
	I can decompose a number into several different yet equivalent sets of bundles or groups of hundreds, tens, and/or ones.	

TOPIC: PLANTS AND THEIR ENVIRONMENT

LEARNING INTENTION: I AM LEARNING ABOUT THE PARTS OF A PLANT AND HOW THEY HELP THE PLANT SURVIVE.

GROWS	CRITERIA AND DESCRIPTORS	GLOWS
How I Can Strengthen My Work	For Learning About the Parts of a Plant and How They Help the Plant Survive	Strong Aspects of My Work
	I can name the parts of a common house plant.	
	I can describe the functions of the parts of a common house plant.	
	I can explain how the parts of a house plant contribute to photosynthesis, reproduction, and specific adaptations.	
	I can hypothesize about the ability of specific plants to survive in specific environments.	

TOPIC: SPEAKING AND LISTENING

LEARNING INTENTION: I AM LEARNING TO EVALUATE A SPEAKER'S POINT OF VIEW, REASONING, AND USE OF EVIDENCE.

GROWS	CRITERIA AND DESCRIPTORS	GLOWS
How I Can Strengthen My Work	For Learning to Evaluate a Speaker's Point of View, Reasoning, and Use of Evidence	Strong Aspects of My Work
	I can identify the role of the narrator/speaker.	
	I can identify the perspective of the speaker.	
	I can identify the reasons that the speaker provides for their perspective.	
	I can identify the evidence that the speaker provides for their perspective.	
	I can determine the credibility of the sources (evidence) that the speaker uses.	
	I can evaluate the overall perspective and determine if I agree that the evidence supports the perspective.	

TOPIC: WORLD HISTORY

LEARNING INTENTION: I AM LEARNING ABOUT ARTISTIC AND ARCHITECTURAL TRADITIONS IN MESO-AMERICAN AND ANDEAN CIVILIZATIONS.

GROWS	CRITERIA AND DESCRIPTORS	GLOWS
How I Can Strengthen My Work	For Learning About Artistic and Architectural Traditions in Meso-American and Andean Civilizations	Strong Aspects of My Work
	I can locate the Meso-American and Andean civilizations in time and place.	
	I can identify the architectural traditions of the region.	
	I can identify the artistic traditions of the region.	
	I can describe the impact of the time and place on the architectural and artistic traditions.	

MODULE 6
CREATING AND IMPLEMENTING RUBRICS

Rubrics allow learners to do the following:

- Have clarity around multifaceted learning intentions that have multiple components for success (e.g., writing a report of information, comparing two historical accounts of the same event).

- Work on different aspects of a process or product at the same time—whether individually or collaboratively, or face-to-face or remotely.

- See the complexity of specific content, practices, and dispositions.

- Receive better feedback that targets specific components of the process or product.

Before you engage with the information in this module, rate yourself on each of the following success criteria using the four-item scale:

- I can explain the key features of both analytic and holistic rubrics.

  Novice 〉Apprentice 〉Practitioner〉 Expert

- I can explain when either an analytic or holistic rubric is useful as a tool for success.

  Novice 〉Apprentice 〉Practitioner〉 Expert

- I can create rubrics aligned to the learning intentions.

  Novice 〉Apprentice 〉Practitioner〉 Expert

- I can use rubrics to organize feedback from peers and from teachers.

  Novice 〉Apprentice 〉Practitioner〉 Expert

A rubric is a set of criteria that, together, articulate what successful completion of a product or performance looks like. Rubrics articulate the criteria for success, descriptors of what success looks like, and the range of levels of success. For example, the successful writing of a laboratory report involves many elements of technical writing (e.g., tone, vocabulary, grammar) and scientific practices (e.g., hypothesizing, analyzing, drawing conclusions). A rubric for successful laboratory writing would contain these elements and descriptors of what success looks like for each level of quality. So, what type of context or situation calls for a rubric over the other options for creating and sharing success criteria?

There are many instances in which success is demonstrated through a performance or the development of a product that assimilates *content*, *practices*, and *dispositions*. Here are some examples:

- Using appropriate tools to strategically develop a solution to a problem
- Constructing an argument
- Developing visual representations of data
- Engaging an audience through writing or speaking
- Communicating scientific phenomena

All of these examples require learners to engage in specific practices, within the context of specific content, while demonstrating certain dispositions. The success criteria in these cases are multifaceted

1. Do my success criteria truly represent the learning intentions for my learners?

2. Did I pick the best option for implementing success criteria based on the type of learning expected of my students?

3. Am I using success criteria to support my students taking ownership of their learning?

> Learners, whether working individually or collaboratively, may be at different points in the progression toward success.

and incorporate multiple components for success. Learners, whether working individually or collaboratively, may be at different points in the progression toward success or working on different aspects of the performance or product. These performances or products can be worked on synchronously or asynchronously, which demands even more clarity around what success looks like for the specific task. When we try to use *I can* or *We can* statements in these situations, we encounter many of the challenges presented in Module 2. The following examples further illustrate some of these challenges.

CHALLENGE	EXAMPLE
Too procedural	We are learning about the relationship between mass and volume so that we can understand density. We'll know we have it when: • We can follow the directions in a laboratory. • We can graph my data. • We can answer questions at the end of the laboratory.
Product-focused	We are learning that the geometric properties of regular shapes are not changed by rigid transformations so that we can better understand congruence and symmetry. We'll know we have it when: • We can create a tessellation.
Not measurable	We are learning about the role of Napoleon in the French Revolution. We'll know we have it when: • We can be sure that the causes of the French Revolution are clear to me.

As illustrated by each of the three examples, *I can* or *We can* statements are not the most clarifying approach to creating and implementing success criteria. Rubrics are a better approach for making the expectations for success clear to our learners. There are two types of rubrics: analytic and holistic. Let's first look at an example of a rubric for successful laboratory writing in science (Figure 6.1).

FIGURE 6.1 Laboratory Report Rubric

		ACCOMPLISHED	DEVELOPING	BEGINNING
1.	**Heading, Neatness, and Organization**	1. The lab report is written in clear and concise language. 2. The sections are clearly marked and sequentially follow the scientific method. 3. The report utilizes appropriate scientific terminology. 4. The report is free of spelling/grammatical errors.	The lab report fails to meet one of the expectations for Headings, Neatness, and Organization.	The lab report fails to meet two or more of the expectations for Headings, Neatness, and Organization.
2.	**Statement of the Problem**	The statement of the problem is in the form of a scientific question and focuses on the scientific phenomenon.	The statement of the problem is focused on the procedural aspects of the lab and not on the scientific phenomenon.	There is no statement of the problem or the statement is not presented in the form of a scientific question.

The Success Criteria Playbook

		ACCOMPLISHED	DEVELOPING	BEGINNING
3.	**Presentation of Scientific Ideas or Concepts**	The ideas or concepts underlying the scientific phenomenon are described using scientific terminology; examples are provided to illustrate the ideas or concepts.	The ideas or concepts are defined and only the procedural aspects of the lab are described; there are no examples provided.	Ideas or concepts underlying the scientific phenomenon are missing from the lab report.
4.	**Procedure**	A full account of the lab is provided to ensure replicability of the experiment.	The procedure is missing key aspects of the lab or focuses on irrelevant details (e.g., fetching glassware, washing glassware); the experiment could be replicated, but with fewer details.	There is minimal or no procedure presented in the lab report; the experiment could not be replicated.
5.	**Data**	1. All data from the experiment are included. 2. Data are organized using tables, graphs, or charts. 3. All data use correct units, labels, and significant figures.	The data section is incomplete (e.g., units, labels on graphs).	The data section is missing from the lab report or unverifiable by an outside peer reviewer.
6.	**Data Analysis**	Data analysis fully addresses the problem statement and utilizes correct descriptive and inferential statistics.	The data analysis does not fully address the problem statement or does not utilize correct descriptive and inferential statistics.	The data section is missing or does not address the problem nor use correct descriptive and inferential statistics.
7.	**Conclusion and Discussion of Results**	The conclusion and discussion describe what can be concluded from the experimental results, directly reference the ideas and concepts associated with the scientific phenomenon, describe possible sources of error, and also describe what would be expected if the experimental data were different.	The conclusion and discussion do not draw direct connections to the experimental results; if in conflict with and/or not supported by the experimental results, there is no discussion of the error (i.e., error analysis).	The conclusion and discussion are missing or are in conflict with and/or not supported by the experimental results.

Source: Adapted from https://studylib.net/doc/7392039/ap-chemistry-lab-rubric.

Figure 6.1 is an example of an analytic rubric. Analytic rubrics provide levels of quality for each element associated with the product or performance. Note that the rubric in Figure 6.1 has seven indicators (down the left side) and three descriptive levels of performance. In this case, there are seven different elements of success that can each be evaluated separately. A learner may meet or exceed expectations for success in analysis (indicator 6) but need additional revising with the concept element (indicator 3).

As another example, consider one of the indicators of the following presentation skills rubric (there are five on the full rubric), and note that it has three descriptive levels of performance.

	EMERGING	DEVELOPING	ADVANCED	COMMENTS
Audience Adaptation	The presenter is not able to keep the audience engaged. The verbal or nonverbal feedback from the audience may suggest a lack of interest or confusion. Topic selection does not relate to audience needs and interests. Delivery is not modified based on audience feedback.	The presenter is able to keep the audience engaged most of the time. When feedback indicates a need for idea clarification, the speaker makes an attempt to clarify or restate ideas. Generally, the speaker demonstrates audience awareness through nonverbal and verbal behaviors. Topic selection and examples are somewhat appropriate for the audience, occasion, or setting.	The presenter is able to effectively keep the audience engaged. Material is modified or clarified as needed given audience verbal and nonverbal feedback. Nonverbal behaviors are used to keep the audience engaged. Delivery style is modified as needed. Topic selection and examples are interesting and relevant for the audience and occasion.	

Another type of rubric is the holistic rubric (Figure 6.2). A holistic rubric does not have different levels of quality for each element associated with a product or performance. For example, if learners engage in a mathematical task that asks them to create and use a model to solve a problem, the holistic rubric would provide a list of expectations associated with success. For learners to demonstrate that they meet or exceed those expectations, they would need to demonstrate all of the expectations within that classification.

FIGURE 6.2 3-Point Holistic Rubric

SCORE	INDICATORS
3 points (A 3-point response is complete and correct.)	• Demonstrates a thorough understanding of the mathematical concepts, practices, and procedures utilized in the task. • Indicates that the student has completed the task correctly, using mathematically sound practices and procedures. • Contains clear, complete explanations and/or adequate work that shows mathematical reasoning.
2 points (A 2-point response is partially correct.)	• Demonstrates a partial understanding of the mathematical concepts, practices, and procedures utilized in the task. • Addresses most aspects of the task, using mathematically sound practices and procedures. • May contain an incorrect solution but applies a mathematically appropriate process with valid reasoning and/or explanation. • May contain a correct solution but provides incomplete procedures, reasoning, and/or explanation. • May reflect some misconceptions of the underlying mathematical concepts, practices, and/or procedures.
1 point (A 1-point response is incomplete and exhibits many flaws but is not completely incorrect.)	• Demonstrates a limited understanding of the mathematical concepts, practices, and procedures embodied in the task. • Addresses elements of the task correctly but reaches an incomplete solution and provides incomplete or incorrect mathematical reasoning. • Exhibits multiple misconceptions related to a misunderstanding of important aspects of the task, misuse of mathematical procedures, or incorrect mathematical reasoning. • Reflects limited understanding of the mathematical concepts of the task. • May contain a correct numerical answer but adequate work that shows mathematical reasoning is not provided.
0 points	• The response is completely incorrect or correct, but it has no supporting work that shows mathematical reasoning.

Source: Adapted from https://studylib.net/doc/5871160/3-point-holistic-rubric—schoolworld-an-edline-solution.

To meet expectations using the rubric in Figure 6.2 and earn 3 points, or whatever point value you use in your holistic rubric, learners would need to demonstrate each element in that row. Rubrics are effective for communicating expectations when there are too many *I can* or *We can* statements. Instead, cluster these statements into broader categories of criteria that represent the *content*, *practices*, and *dispositions* included in the specific performance or product.

> Rubrics are effective for communicating expectations when there are too many *I can* or *We can* statements.

YOUR TURN!

Before we work through the process for generating success criteria through analytic and holistic rubrics, take a few moments to compare and contrast the two types of rubrics. In your comparing and contrasting, focus on when you and your colleagues might select one rubric type over the other.

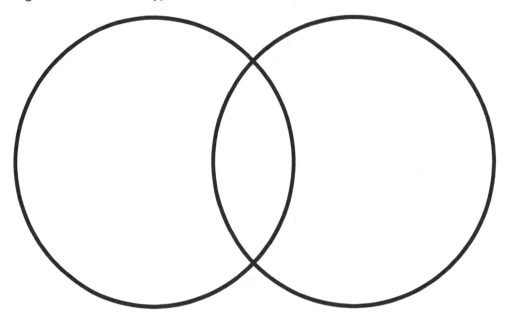

For upcoming learning experiences where an analytic or holistic rubric is the best way to know and show success criteria, list the learning intentions in the space provided. Use the space in the second column to identify which type of rubric and the third to describe why. We will come back to this information soon. For now, just be thinking about which type of rubric you might use to communicate the success criteria and why.

LEARNING INTENTIONS	ANALYTIC OR HOLISTIC	WHY?

HOW DO WE GENERATE ANALYTIC OR HOLISTIC RUBRICS?

Although there is no one right way to build an analytic or holistic rubric, the following guidelines are helpful in ensuring that the rubric allows learners to answer the question: *How will I know when I am successful?*

GUIDELINES FOR GENERATING RUBRICS

- Develop a clear understanding of the assigned product, project, or performance. What content, practices, and dispositions would demonstrate success in this product, project, or performance? What would a successful product, project, or performance look like? These become our criteria. Using the science example in Figure 6.1, these criteria include (1) heading, neatness, and organization, (2) statement of the problem, (3) presentation of scientific ideas or concepts, (4) procedure, (5) data, (6) data analysis, and (7) conclusion and discussion of results.

- Select the type of rubric that best fits the assigned product, project, or performance (i.e., analytic or holistic). Does the learner need to demonstrate success on all the criteria at the same time or can there be differential success?

- Identify the descriptors for each criterion that will make the product, project, or performance proficient. This should be perfectly aligned with the learning intention and not incorporate irrelevant details (e.g., handwriting, unmeasurable qualities). Furthermore, is this an individual endeavor or can we leverage individual learning through collective learning? This determines whether we use *I* or *We* in the rubrics.

- Step up and identify the criteria that will make the product, project, or performance an exemplar or exceed expectations. What would be above and beyond expectations?

- Step down and identify the criteria that will make the product, project, or performance "progressing" or "not yet." This should be based on where learners might need additional support or experience to meet expectations. Again, this should focus on learning, not irrelevant details.

Notice that high-quality criteria and descriptors for both the analytic and holistic rubrics seem to have the same characteristics as high-quality *I can* or *We can* statements. Return to page 61 in Module 4. Write those characteristics in the following box using the different sentence stem.

HIGH-QUALITY CRITERIA AND DESCRIPTORS IN MY RUBRICS SHOULD:

The similarity between *I can* statements and criteria and descriptors in rubrics is not coincidental. Remember, both are success criteria in different forms.

GUIDED PRACTICE

For the following processes and products, develop either an analytic or holistic rubric. When finished, please turn to page 107 for sample answers.

- **Mathematics:** Construct a viable mathematical argument (e.g., proportional reasoning and looking for and expressing regularity in repeated reasoning [MP8])
- **Science:** Construct valid arguments and critique the reasoning of others
- **English Language Arts:** Writing a report of information
- **Social Studies:** Compare two historical accounts of the same event

HOLISTIC RUBRIC TEMPLATE

LEVELS OF SUCCESS	CRITERIA AND DESCRIPTORS
Exceeds Expectations	
Meets Expectations	
Still Working	

ANALYTIC RUBRIC TEMPLATE

CRITERIA	STILL WORKING	MEETS EXPECTATIONS	EXCEEDS EXPECTATIONS

YOUR TURN!

Select a learning intention that involves a performance or product or requires too many *I can* or *We can* statements. Develop an analytic or holistic rubric. Maybe you and your colleagues have multiple learning intentions that would allow you to build an analytic rubric (e.g., compare two historical accounts of the same event, gather compelling scientific evidence) and a holistic rubric (e.g., construct a viable mathematical argument, use text features to make meaning). To build your rubrics, download the templates and reproducibles provided at resources.corwin.com/successcriteriaplaybook

PATHWAY TO EQUITY: HOW DO WE GET *ALL* LEARNERS TO ENGAGE WITH RUBRICS?

Rubrics can be overwhelming. Plus, as learners engage in the learning, they may forget to return to the rubric for guidance about knowing and showing their learning. The evidence on rubrics clearly indicates that they must be introduced early and not be left until the end and thus be used for evaluation alone. For students to use the rubrics to monitor their progress and focus their learning in any context, they need to understand the rubric (success criteria) at the outset of their learning (Brookhart, 2013).

> For students to use the rubrics to monitor their progress and focus their learning in any context, they need to understand the rubric at the outset of their learning.

YOUR TURN!

So, how will you engage your learners in rubrics and ensure they continue to use them in their work? Use the space provided to map out a plan for creating and implementing rubrics in your classroom or through your remote learning platform. Be sure to add your own ideas to our list if you feel like a strategy is missing or if you have one that works for you but is not on our list.

WALK THROUGH THE RUBRIC BEFORE RELEASING STUDENTS TO ENGAGE IN THE WORK.

DEVELOP GUIDING QUESTIONS TO ASK LEARNERS THAT REQUIRE THEM TO RETURN TO THE RUBRIC.

IMPLEMENT A PEER FEEDBACK OR PEER EVALUATION STEP BEFORE LEARNERS COMPLETE THE PROJECT OR PERFORMANCE.

IMPLEMENT A SELF-CHECK STEP BEFORE LEARNERS COMPLETE THE PROJECT OR PERFORMANCE.

BUILD IN CHECK-INS (DURING THE LEARNING EXPERIENCE AND AT THE END OF EACH DAY OR SEGMENT).

Now that you have finished this module, rate yourself on each of the following success criteria using the four-item scale. Use the space provided at the end to self-reflect on your own learning. What will you do next with this information? You may not yet be at the expert level, as it takes time to integrate knowledge into practice. Use this information to identify areas of continued learning.

- I can explain the key features of both analytic and holistic rubrics.

- I can explain when either an analytic or holistic rubric is useful as a tool for success.

- I can create rubrics aligned to the learning intentions.

- I can use rubrics to organize feedback from peers and from teachers.

SUGGESTED ANSWERS FOR MODULE 6

ANALYTIC RUBRIC TEMPLATE FOR MIDDLE SCHOOL MATHEMATICS EXAMPLE

Construct a Viable Mathematical Argument

CRITERIA	STILL WORKING	MEETS EXPECTATIONS	EXCEEDS EXPECTATIONS
I can describe the relationship between two quantities or measures that creates a ratio.	I can describe the two quantities or measures separately but I'm not sure how they're related or how they create a ratio.	I can describe why the two quantities are related to create a ratio.	I can describe why the two quantities are related to create a ratio and how changes in each quantity would affect the ratio.
I can represent and explain the ratio using the context, images, mathematical language, and notation.	I can create a single representation of the ratio and explain it using the context, images, mathematical language, or notation. I am working on explaining the meaning of the ratio using all four criteria: context, images, mathematical language, and notation.	I can create one or two representations of the ratio and explain them using the context, images, mathematical language, and notation.	I can create multiple representations to show the meaning of the ratio and explain the relationships between the representations, using the context, images, mathematical language, and notation.
I can look for and express regularity in repeated reasoning to identify and create the ratio.	I can see relationships between the two quantities or measures but I'm not sure how to describe the pattern or repeated reasoning that creates a ratio.	I can see and describe the relationship between the two quantities or measures and I can represent and explain the pattern or repeated reasoning that creates the ratio.	I can generalize the repeated reasoning that creates the ratio between the two quantities or measures and apply it to new, related contexts.
I can use the ratio to problem solve and evaluate the reasonableness of my solution.	I can start to extend the pattern but I'm not sure how to make large jumps using the ratio. I'm working on making sense of the relationship between the two quantities or measures in order to evaluate the reasonableness of my solution.	I can apply the ratio to extend the pattern to any term. I can use my understanding of the ratio and my representations to defend the reasonableness of my solution.	I can justify the reasonableness of my generalization by explaining whether the ratio is a part-to-part ratio, a part-to-whole ratio, a quotient, or a rate.

CONTINUED

CONTINUED

ANALYTIC RUBRIC TEMPLATE FOR ELEMENTARY SCIENCE EXAMPLE

Construct Valid Arguments and Critique the Reasoning of Others

CRITERIA	3	2	1
I can make a scientifically accurate claim.	My claim is scientifically accurate and is consistent with the scientific investigation.	My claim is scientifically accurate, but is not directly related to the scientific investigation.	My claim is not scientifically accurate.
I can provide evidence to support my claim.	My claim is supported by more than two pieces of evidence from the investigation.	My claim is supported by one or two pieces of evidence, but not related to the scientific investigation.	My claim is not supported by evidence from the scientific investigation.
I can explain that my evidence supports my claim.	My explanation makes a direct connection between the claim and the supporting evidence from the investigation.	My explanation makes connections between my claim and only some of the evidence from the investigation.	My explanation does not make a connection between my claim and evidence from the investigation.
I can respond to questions and comments from my peers.	My explanation incorporates questions and comments from my peers.	My explanation incorporates only questions and comments from my teacher.	My explanation does not incorporate questions or comments from my peers or teacher.

ANALYTIC RUBRIC FOR ENGLISH LANGUAGE ARTS EXAMPLE

Use Text Features to Make Meaning

	RATING				SCORE
	4	3	2	1	
Introduction	The topic is clearly introduced with highlights of information to come. The reader is hooked.	The topic is introduced. There is limited information about what is to come. The reader is interested.	The topic is introduced. There is no information about the information that will be shared. The reader is unsure.	The topic is not introduced. The paper starts with the information that is not organized. The reader is confused.	
Organization	Well organized, demonstrates logical sequencing and structure.	Well organized, but demonstrates illogical sequencing or structure.	Weakly organized with no logical sequencing or structure.	No organization, sequencing, or structure.	

	RATING				SCORE
	4	3	2	1	
Conclusions	Detailed conclusions are reached from the evidence offered.	Conclusions are reached from the evidence offered.	There is some indication of conclusions from the evidence offered.	No conclusions are made from the evidence offered.	
Sources	Information is gathered from five or more credible sources. Sources are cited appropriately.	Information is gathered from two to four credible sources. Sources are cited properly, but one or more are missing or not used.	Information is gathered from a single credible source. Source is cited, but has errors.	The information is not credible. Sources are not cited or are cited incorrectly.	
Mechanics	The conventions of language are appropriate for the topic and minimal errors are evident.	The conventions are generally correct but errors are noted.	The conventions are problematic and distract the reader.	The mechanics prevent the reader from understanding.	
TOTAL POINTS					

HOLISTIC RUBRIC FOR SOCIAL STUDIES EXAMPLE

Compare Two Historical Accounts of the Same Event

SCORE	INDICATORS
2 points	• Two accounts are introduced. • Both accounts are considered in the narrative. • Comparison includes similarities and differences. • Organizational structure (text-by-text or point-by-point) is evident. • Basis and/or perspective is discussed. • Conclusions are supported from the evidence presented.
1 point	• Two accounts are introduced. • Comparison focuses mainly on one account or the other. • Potential bias or perspectives is recognized and named. • Conclusions include summarizing statements.
0 points	• One account is introduced. • The focus in on one perspective. • Bias and perspective are not noted.

NOTES

MODULE 7: CREATING & IMPLEMENTATION
through TEACHER MODELING
Showing & KNOWING
TALK IS NOT!
THINKING IS INVISIBLE...
"HERE'S HOW I THINK ABOUT IT..."
HERE'S HOW TO DO IT...
THE PLAY:
EXPLICIT MODELING AS A CLEAR, MULTI-SENSORY MODEL OF SUCCESS
THE CALL:
ARE LEARNING INTENTIONS
✓ HIGHLY COMPLEX?
✓ ABSTRACT?
ARE LEARNERS:
✓ NEW TO CONCEPT?
✓ NEW READERS?
✓ LANGUAGE LEARNERS?

MODULE 7
CREATING AND IMPLEMENTING SUCCESS CRITERIA THROUGH TEACHER MODELING

Teacher modeling allows learners to do the following:

- Know and show success criteria when the learning intentions involve highly complex or abstract ideas, concepts, or processes.

- Be introduced to the success criteria for the first time.

- Strengthen their literacy and academic language skills (e.g., particularly young learners, English language learners, students with processing or reading disabilities).

Before you engage with the information in this module, rate yourself on each of the following success criteria using the four-item scale:

- I can describe the essential features of teacher modeling.

| Novice | Apprentice | Practitioner | Expert |

- I can explain the ways in which teacher modeling helps students know what success looks like.

| Novice | Apprentice | Practitioner | Expert |

- I can design modeling opportunities for students that ensure they understand success in terms of *content*, *practices*, and *dispositions*.

| Novice | Apprentice | Practitioner | Expert |

- I can engage learners while modeling for them.

| Novice | Apprentice | Practitioner | Expert |

The complexities of learning are not always clear in written form. For example, expectations for learners to use different models to represent equivalent fractions in mathematics or draw a free-body diagram in physics are measurable and actionable, but they require learners to engage with highly abstract ideas. In English language arts, constructing a viable argument or comparing information from two sources is not easily reduced to a checklist. Learning to make inferences or write poetry is nuanced, highly contextualized, and cognitively demanding. Historians consider bias and perspective and the credibility of sources, each of which can be modeled for students using different primary source documents. The specific actions (use models, draw free-body diagrams, make a prediction based on what is known, or consider bias) can still be nebulous to learners, not because of poorly written success criteria but because of the content's complexity, the novelty of success criteria to the learner, or the learner's reading proficiency. Nothing else could be added to these statements to enhance the clarity of the success criteria.

Teacher modeling aims to address these challenges, and it is a strong approach for the following:

- Knowing and showing success criteria when the learning intentions involve highly complex or abstract ideas, concepts, or processes

- Introducing learners to the success criteria for the first time

- Strengthening learners' literacy and academic language skills (e.g., particularly young learners, English language learners, students with processing or reading disabilities).

The purpose of explicit teacher modeling is to provide students with a clear, multisensory model of what success looks like in these types of situations. Modeling allows teachers to open up their brains and explain how they think. Thinking is invisible. But we can *talk about* our thinking.

> The purpose of explicit teacher modeling is to provide students with a clear, multisensory model of what success looks like.

Teacher modeling works for *content*, *practices*, and *dispositions*. Let's look at some examples. The following success criteria are difficult to capture using only written statements and are best represented through teacher modeling.

	MATHEMATICS	SCIENCE	ENGLISH LANGUAGE ARTS	HISTORY
Content	Explain the concept of a ratio and associated unit rates and use ratio language to describe proportional relationships.	Evaluate changes in the understanding of the solar system over time as changes in technology provided more information.	Draw on information from multiple print or digital sources, demonstrating the ability to locate an answer to a question quickly or to solve a problem efficiently.	Describe the relationship between the moral and political ideas of the Great Awakening and the development of revolutionary fervor.
Practices	Notice patterns in multiplying and dividing odd and even numbers in order to evaluate the reasonableness of solutions.	Use a model to predict the relationships between systems or between components of a system.	Apply grade-level phonics knowledge and word analysis skills in decoding.	Recognize the role of chance, oversight, and error in history.
Dispositions	Use a mistake as an opportunity to learn by analyzing why the mistake makes sense and why it does not work.	Communicate scientific ideas (e.g., about phenomena) in multiple formats (including orally, graphically, textually, and mathematically).	Seek feedback from others and revise writing accordingly.	Persist in seeking clarity about bias and perspective in historical documents.

1. Do my success criteria truly represent the learning intentions for my learners?

2. Did I pick the best option for implementing success criteria based on the type of learning expected of my students?

3. Am I using success criteria to support my students taking ownership of their learning?

In each of the situations described, we recognize that *I can* or *We can* statements and single-point, analytic, and holistic rubrics alone may not provide enough clarity for learners to know what success looks like. Teacher modeling can be paired with other written forms of success criteria, or it can be used as the only way of knowing and showing the success criteria. Through teacher modeling, we would do the following:

1. Describe and model the content, practice, and/or disposition.

2. Explain the thinking behind the thinking, or meta-cognition, so that students know both how and why something is done.

3. Clearly highlight the content while performing the practice and applying the disposition.

4. Ensure that the modeling breaks down the content, practice, and/or disposition into manageable components.

5. Use multiple modes (e.g., verbal cues, images, graphics, and gestures).

Our thinking is typically invisible to students; teacher modeling makes it visible. Modeling for students enables them to makes sense of the task and the process for mastering the success criteria.

YOUR TURN!

Are there specific concepts, practices, or ideas that require you to "show" learners what success looks like? Are your students being introduced to the idea of success criteria for one of the first times? For example, do you have students who are still learning to read? Do you have students who are still learning to read? If so, teacher modeling may be the best approach for knowing and showing success criteria. With your colleagues, develop a list of success criteria for an upcoming lesson, or series of lessons, that you believe will require teacher modeling. List them in the first column of the following chart. Then, think about how you will model the outcome or outcomes using the five characteristics just mentioned. Just discuss the questions in the column on the right. We will map out a plan in the next Your Turn.

SUCCESS CRITERIA	USING THE FIVE CHARACTERISTICS, HOW WILL YOU MODEL THE SUCCESS CRITERIA?
	1. How will you describe or model success? 2. How will you explain the thinking behind the thinking? 3. What content will you highlight? 4. How will you break down the content, practice, or disposition? 5. What multiple modes will you use?
	1. How will you describe or model success? 2. How will you explain the thinking behind the thinking? 3. What content will you highlight? 4. How will you break down the content, practice, or disposition? 5. What multiple modes will you use?
	1. How will you describe or model success? 2. How will you explain the thinking behind the thinking? 3. What content will you highlight? 4. How will you break down the content, practice, or disposition? 5. What multiple modes will you use?

online resources ⬐ Available for download at **resources.corwin.com/successcriteriaplaybook**

HOW DO WE GENERATE TEACHER MODELING?

Although teacher modeling may seem routine to us, the implementation of this approach for creating and sharing success criteria requires very intentional planning and preparation. As teachers, we have a higher level of comfort with the content, practices, and dispositions. Often, our thinking is on autopilot because we have developed proficiency with the content. Therefore, we can easily leave out a detail in the modeling process that seems obvious to us, but it may not be so obvious to students

> We can easily leave out a detail in the modeling process that seems obvious to us, but it may not be so obvious to students encountering this learning for the very first time.

encountering this learning for the very first time. We have to generate our modeling by taking the learner's perspective. This requires us to examine our expert blind spots and remember what it is like to learn this content. What do students need to see and hear to clearly understand what the expectations are for the day's learning?

GUIDELINES FOR TEACHER MODELING

- Identify the specific success criteria that need modeling.
- Break down the content, practices, and dispositions.
- Develop and practice how you will describe the content, practices, and/or dispositions.
- Develop and practice how you will model the content, practices, and/or dispositions.
- Develop your visual, tactile, auditory, or kinesthetic modalities of representation.
- When engaged in the teacher modeling, think aloud to let the learners see your processing and thinking about the content, practices, and/or dispositions. Ask yourself, *What do I do and what do I think as I perform the practice? What decisions do I make? When might I make a mistake that is typical of my learners?*
- Use *I* statements rather than *You* or *We* statements when modeling for students.
- Develop both examples and non-examples to include in the modeling.
- Highlight or emphasize specific cues that lead to you making certain decisions about where to go next.

GUIDED PRACTICE

Offering opportunities for guided practice with teacher modeling is not possible in a book. However, practicing teacher modeling with your colleagues and then getting feedback on your modeling is very effective. Another option is to find video clips online that show teachers modeling success criteria. As a PLC+, use the features of teacher modeling and the guidelines for setting up teacher modeling and engage in an analysis of a video clip. Use the following guiding questions to facilitate the analysis:

1. When engaged in the teacher modeling, did the teacher think aloud to let the learners see their processing and thinking about the content, practices, and/or dispositions? Did the teacher reflectively share the following: *What do I do and what do I think as I perform the practice? What decisions do I make? When might I make a mistake that is typical of my learners?*

2. Did the teacher use *I* statements rather than *You* or *We* statements when modeling for students?

3. Did the teacher develop and use both examples and non-examples in the modeling?

4. Did the teacher highlight or emphasize specific cues that led to them making certain decisions about where to go next in their thinking?

The Success Criteria Playbook

YOUR TURN!

Return to the previous Your Turn! exercise on page 115 in this module. Take the work you did with your colleagues and move forward with creating a teacher modeling session. Using the guidelines for teacher modeling presented earlier in this module, intentionally plan out the details. Use the following space to develop your teacher modeling.

SUCCESS CRITERIA	USING THE GUIDELINES, PLAN FOR TEACHER MODELING

PATHWAY TO EQUITY: HOW DO WE GET *ALL* LEARNERS TO ENGAGE WITH TEACHER MODELING?

Getting learners to engage with teacher modeling can be difficult. There is only so much information a student can absorb before reaching cognitive overload. So, we need to ensure that learners attend to the right information. Just because we are modeling the success criteria for our learners does not mean they are paying attention to the most relevant information in the model or that they are paying attention at all. To ensure learners engage with our modeling, we should keep a few things in mind.

> There is only so much information a student can absorb before reaching cognitive overload.

1. *Provide a meaningful context for the modeling* (e.g., a contextualized problem that is authentic and relevant to learners, a demonstration/discrepant event). By providing a context, we increase the chances that learners will buy into and be motivated to pay attention to the relevant details. This requires the contextualized problem or demonstration to align with the learning outcomes.

2. *Ensure that there are visual, tactile, auditory, or kinesthetic modalities of representation in the modeling.* Make sure to visually display any equation, word problem, text, cycle, illustration, or celestial object. Include concrete objects when possible and model transforming them into a diagram or sketch. We can even adjust our auditory components by orally cuing students through varying vocal intonations. Kinesthetically point, circle, highlight, and/or label computation signs or important information on the interactive whiteboard or screen. We can perform each of these components remotely by sharing our screen, using a virtual laser pointer, and/or animating our graphic as we engage in the modeling.

3. *Think aloud.* Make sure we let learners see our thinking at key decision points and how we resolve our own conflicts or struggles in the learning. Using *I* statements invites them into our thinking and reduces the cognitive demand for students.

4. *Explicitly make connections.* Do not leave important connections to chance. As we engage with learners, we must directly connect each action with the specific content, practices, or dispositions we want our learners to notice. For example, we can restate what we did in the previous step, what we are going to do in the next step, and why the next step is important to the previous step.

> Do not leave important connections to chance.

5. *Bring learners into the modeling experience.* Use formative assessments, questioning, or checks for understanding to ensure learners are focusing on the relevant and important aspects of the modeling. In breakout rooms through a virtual environment, have learners develop a collective list of aspects that need additional explanation. Remodel steps when there is uncertainty or confusion.

6. *Monitor the pace or speed of the modeling.* Although we want to move at a pace that keeps learners engaged, we have to make sure we do not move too fast. This is particularly important for students learning remotely. Maintain a lively pace while being conscious of student information processing difficulties (e.g., additional time needed to process questions). A modeling session should be no more

than 10 minutes. If possible, record the session and make the recording available to learners.

7. *Multiple exposures.* Expect to model the content, practices, or dispositions more than once over the duration of the lesson or unit. Learners may need multiple exposures to identify the essential details.

YOUR TURN!

As we close out this module, take a moment to map out how you will get your learners to engage in teacher modeling. Use the space provided to map out a plan for creating and implementing teacher modeling in your classroom or through your remote learning platform. Be sure to add your own ideas to our list.

Now that you have finished this module, rate yourself on each of the following success criteria using the four-item scale. Use the space provided at the end to self-reflect on your own learning. What will you do next with this information? You may not yet be at the expert level, as it takes time to integrate knowledge into practice. Use this information to identify areas of continued learning.

- I can describe the essential features of teacher modeling.

- I can explain the ways in which teacher modeling helps students know what success looks like.

- I can design modeling opportunities for students that ensure they understand success in terms of *content*, *practices*, and *dispositions*.

- I can engage learners while modeling for them.

The Success Criteria Playbook

MODULE 8
CREATING AND IMPLEMENTING SUCCESS CRITERIA THROUGH EXEMPLARS

Exemplars allow learners to do the following:

- Self-monitor, self-evaluate, and self-reflect on their learning progress based on the exemplar.
- Transform possibly unclear, abstract expectations into concrete form.
- Use a standard of comparison to focus on areas needing improvement.

Before you engage with the information in this module, rate yourself on each of the following success criteria using the four-item scale:

- I can define exemplars and how they can be used to ensure students know what success looks like.

| Novice | Apprentice | Practitioner | Expert |

- I can explain the way exemplars are developed.

| Novice | Apprentice | Practitioner | Expert |

- I can justify the use of exemplars for specific learning intentions.

| Novice | Apprentice | Practitioner | Expert |

- I can engage students using exemplars and ensure that they understand what success looks like.

| Novice | Apprentice | Practitioner | Expert |

A variation of teacher modeling is the use of exemplars. Instead of the teacher "acting out" the expectations, exemplars are work samples created by previous learners or developed by the teacher (sometimes co-created as a class) to provide a concrete representation of success. By definition, an exemplar is a model that serves as a typical or excellent illustration of processes, tasks, or products. An exemplar is not just any example or non-example. An exemplar should possess the essential characteristics of work that meets all the criteria for success.

1. Do my success criteria truly represent the learning intentions for my learners?

2. Did I pick the best option for implementing success criteria based on the type of learning expected of my students?

3. Am I using success criteria to support my students taking ownership of their learning?

YOUR TURN!

There are pros and cons to using exemplars. What do you think they are? Take a few moments and develop a list of these pros and cons in the space provided.

PROS	CONS

You likely identified several benefits to using exemplars. For example, learners can use models to self-monitor, self-evaluate, and self-reflect on their learning progress. Exemplars can transform possibly unclear, abstract expectations into concrete form. Finally, exemplars provide a standard of comparison for learners to focus on areas needing improvement. This can be done in the classroom or through a remote learning platform. Here are some examples:

- In elementary mathematics, we can use exemplars to make clear how we can translate concrete manipulatives (like base-ten blocks) into labeled sketches, charts, and equations in order to show the actions of decomposing and composing two-digit numbers for addition and subtraction.

- In high school geometry, we can use exemplars to show what we mean by a rigorous and elegant proof for a geometric theorem that has multiple representations (including labeled diagrams, equations, and written statements) woven throughout.

- In the elementary science classroom, we can use exemplars to guide learners as they record observations in their interactive notebooks (e.g., measurements, the water cycle, illustrations of the parts of a flower).

- In high school science, we can use exemplars that clarify what we mean by developing, revising, and/or using a model based on evidence to illustrate and/or predict the relationships between systems or between components of a system (e.g., cell processes, ecosystems, complex machines, weather patterns).

- In elementary English language arts, we can use student writing exemplars to note effective transitions between paragraphs.

- In high school English language arts, we can study published authors as exemplars of introduction styles or dialogue.

- In middle school social studies, we can use exemplars to show what it means to create a visual display of information, such as the organization of city-states in Ancient Greece.

- In high school social studies, we can provide exemplars of a prior year's students analysis of United States Supreme Court Cases to highlight the level of analysis expected in the performance task.

Although exemplars have many benefits, they also have drawbacks. To develop a library of exemplars, a significant amount of time is required to evaluate student work and decide if the characteristics of the process, task, or product meet the standards necessary to be a model. Plus, we have to ensure that other students are okay with having their work used as an exemplar. One additional concern that often accompanies exemplars has to do with creativity and plagiarism. Does the use of an exemplar encourage learners to play it safe or simply replicate the exemplar? We are not looking for 30 replicas of the exemplar.

YOUR TURN!

Consider the following expectations. What differences in expectations make some more suited for exemplars, while others might suppress creativity and lead to plagiarism? We will discuss these examples next.

LEARNING INTENTION	WHAT WOULD LEARNERS SAY AND DO IF THEY HAVE MASTERED THE LEARNING INTENTION?	IS AN EXEMPLAR APPROPRIATE? (YES OR NO)	WHY?
1. I am learning that inverse functions model relationships between two quantities.	• Identify a situation where two quantities change in an inverse relationship to one another. • Use multiple representations to show this relationship.		
2. I am learning to use what I know about slope and intercept to interpret linear functions within data contexts.	• Identify the slope and interpret its meaning within the data. • Identify the intercept and interpret its meaning within the data. • Explain the trends of the data based on the line of best fit.		

LEARNING INTENTION	WHAT WOULD LEARNERS SAY AND DO IF THEY HAVE MASTERED THE LEARNING INTENTION?	IS AN EXEMPLAR APPROPRIATE? (YES OR NO)	WHY?
3. I am learning about the parts of a cell.	• Construct a model of a cell. • Describe the parts and function of those parts using the model.		
4. I am learning that habitats include the essential characteristics necessary to support an animal of your choice.	• Identify the essential characteristics of a habitat. • Explain why they are considered essential.		
5. I am learning to retell stories.	• Tell the story in order, beginning, middle, and end. • Include key details from the text.		
6. I am learning to identify who is telling the story at different places in the text.	• Identify the character speaking.		
7. I am learning to identify places on the globe.	• Find the North and South Poles. • Find the equator and the prime meridian. • Locate the tropics and hemispheres. Use coordinates to plot location.		
8. I am learning about the experiences of the settlers on the overland trails to the West.	• Describe the location of the routes. • Discuss the influence of the terrain. • Discuss the influence of the climate. • Describe the obstacles encountered.		

For the mathematics examples, using exemplars would support the learning intention and success criteria in example 1. However, exemplars would narrow or hinder the learning intention and success criteria in example 2, which focus on learners' initial understandings of mathematical topics such as slope and intercept. Learners are just beginning to demonstrate knowledge and comprehension of the language, symbols, and operations. Exemplars at this initial level of understanding could create closed expectations, implying there are limited ways to meet the learning intention and creating the perception of singular right answers. Learners may treat the exemplar and the new task as a fill-in-the-blank or plug-and-chug situation where they simply replace numbers without making sense of the situation, mathematical language, or representations.

Science examples 3 and 4 also provide a contrast. Example 3 requires more discrete knowledge and would thus not necessarily benefit from an exemplar. But example 4 has many options and possibilities, so an example of success would likely be useful.

English language arts example 5 would likely benefit from an exemplar, whereas example 6 would not. The complexity between these examples differs, and example 6 could easily be accomplished with *I can* statements.

Finally, social studies example 7 has clearly right and wrong answers. Exemplars would thus give away the information and students could simply replicate the examples. Example 8, however, requires analysis of several factors or considerations, and an exemplar could show students how to consider the information without inviting them to replicate the exemplar.

Exemplars may remove the learners' opportunities to make decisions and create the implication that they simply need to copy the exemplar. Conversely, exemplars can enhance students' vision for successful mastery of the learning

intentions when they show possibilities and not just one way to accomplish something. At this depth of understanding, learners can use exemplars to analyze the open-endedness of the success criteria. With a focus on connecting many ideas and demonstrating deep understanding, exemplars can highlight the decision points rather than narrow them. While the exemplar may demonstrate one possible path, the exemplar also contributes to the sense of accessible possibility and choice. The exemplar makes the many options manageable by illuminating one route among many routes for comparison and analysis. Although the concerns about suppressing creativity and encouraging the replication of the exemplar are valid, they are avoidable if exemplars are used for the right aspect of understanding (i.e., interpretation, application, perspective, empathizing, and self-knowledge).

> Exemplars can highlight the decision points rather than narrow them.

HOW DO WE GENERATE EXEMPLARS?

Exemplars are generated just as we have generated the previous four approaches to knowing and showing success. First, we must recognize which success criteria are best shared using an exemplar. As we illustrated in the earlier Your Turn! exercise (see page 124), these expectations should provide learners with significant choices so that there is not a natural pull to stifle creativity and simply replicate the model. Then, we must make the crucial decision about whether we are using student work samples as exemplars or developing our own. For student work samples, we will need to devote time to screen each sample and ensure that the characteristics of the work sample align with the expectations or success criteria. If we are developing the exemplars, we must devote time to doing so. We can co-create exemplars with our class. This can be the *we do* part of the gradual release model. Sometimes co-created exemplars are called *anchor charts*.

We can co-create exemplars with our class. This can be the *we do* part of the gradual release model.

GUIDED PRACTICE

Once again, offering opportunities for guided practice with exemplars is no easier than offering guided practice for teacher modeling. This time, to provide an opportunity for you to practice with your colleagues and then get feedback on your use of exemplars, gather several potential exemplars that you can use in your classroom or through your virtual learning platform. Analyze those exemplars and how you will implement them in your teaching. Use the following guiding questions to facilitate the analysis:

1. Does the exemplar possess all of the necessary and essential elements of success?

2. Are those elements easily observed by the learner?

3. Does the particular exemplar represent the abstract or highly complex idea?

4. What level of support will be needed to ensure that learners use the exemplar to help them know what success looks like (e.g., questioning, thinking aloud)?

YOUR TURN!

List the success criteria for an upcoming lesson or series of lessons. Think through the features an exemplar must have to provide a clear and concrete representation of success.

SUCCESS CRITERIA	WHAT CHARACTERISTICS MUST THE EXEMPLAR HAVE?	WILL THIS COME FROM STUDENT WORK SAMPLES OR BE TEACHER CREATED?
Example: Construct a valid argument, recognizing counterarguments, about a topic relevant to our course of study.		

CONTINUED

CONTINUED

SUCCESS CRITERIA	WHAT CHARACTERISTICS MUST THE EXEMPLAR HAVE?	WILL THIS COME FROM STUDENT WORK SAMPLES OR BE TEACHER CREATED?

Before moving on, we want to note that exemplars work for both individual and collective learning. We can provide exemplars that represent what learners are expected to know and be able to do as a result of a collaborative learning experience. When sharing the exemplars with our learners, we can use the exemplars to model what *you* or *we* will be expected to know and show.

PATHWAY TO EQUITY: HOW DO WE GET *ALL* LEARNERS TO ENGAGE WITH EXEMPLARS?

Exemplars work only if our learners notice and use the essential characteristics to inform their decisions about learning. There are several approaches for engaging learners in exemplars:

1. *Analyze the exemplars at the start of the learning experience.* Using probing and clarifying questions, we can help learners see what makes something an exemplar. Having a discussion where learners point out or discuss particular features of exemplars will help them use exemplars as a concrete representation of success criteria. Features generated during this analysis and discussion can be recorded using Padlet or Google Docs.

2. *Place them in interactive notebooks (spiral-bound or digital).* We can ask learners to write the features or characteristics of the exemplars in their interactive notebooks for referencing throughout the learning experience. Then, learners can refer to them and monitor their own learning as they work.

3. *Return to the exemplars during the lesson and use them as a formative assessment or check for understanding.* As we move through the learning experience, we can ask our learners to take time to compare their work to the exemplars to decide where to go next or identify where they may need additional work and time.

4. *Use them at the end of the day as a self-monitoring exit ticket.* We can return to the exemplars and use them for reflection and closure. When exemplars are used in an exit ticket (e.g., paper-and-pencil, Mentimeter), we can see if learners are truly able to demonstrate the expectations represented by the exemplars. This provides valuable information about where to start tomorrow.

YOUR TURN!

As we close out this module, take a moment to map out how you will get your learners to engage with exemplars. Use the space provided to map out a plan for creating and implementing exemplars in your classroom or through your remote learning platform. Be sure to add your own ideas to our list.

Now that you have finished this module, rate yourself on each of the following success criteria using the four-item scale. Use the space provided at the end to self-reflect on your own learning. What will you do next with this information? You may not yet be at the expert level, as it takes time to integrate knowledge into practice. Use this information to identify areas of continued learning.

- I can define exemplars and how they can be used to ensure students know what success looks like.

- I can explain the way exemplars are developed.

- I can justify the use of exemplars for specific learning intentions.

- I can engage students using exemplars and ensure that they understand what success looks like.

MODULE 9
CO-CONSTRUCTING CRITERIA FOR SUCCESS

Co-constructing success criteria allows learners to do the following:

- Experience a truly student-centered approach to success criteria.

- Enhance task relevancy.

- See the purpose and importance in learning and increase their sense of confidence that they can meet expectations.

- Develop their capacity to independently construct success criteria to meet their goals in new contexts both in and out of school.

Before you engage with the information in this module, rate yourself on each of the following success criteria using the four-item scale:

- I can describe ways to co-construct success criteria with students.

  Novice Apprentice Practitioner Expert

- I can identify the information I would need as fodder for the co-construction of success criteria.

  Novice Apprentice Practitioner Expert

- I can explain when the co-construction of success criteria is most likely to be effective.

  Novice Apprentice Practitioner Expert

- I can place the various ways for ensuring students know what success looks like along a continuum from most to least teacher control and responsibility.

  Novice Apprentice Practitioner Expert

The final approach for knowing and showing success criteria involves a truly collaborative effort between teachers and students. Utilizing class work samples, previously made anchor charts, and collections of learners' individual work as the starting point, co-constructing success criteria involves learners analyzing the samples and developing a set of success criteria based on what they identify as the essential characteristics of the samples. Through critical conversations, learners engage in academic discourse about the following:

- The features of the samples
- Why they think those features or characteristics are relevant
- How to transform these characteristics into *I can* statements, *We can* statements, a single-point rubric, or an analytic/holistic rubric

Co-constructing success criteria truly embraces learners as partners in the learning process. In mathematics, the teacher could have learners sort their work midway in their fractions unit to find samples of using models to prove fraction comparisons and equivalencies. The teacher would ask questions to guide the learners' reflections in order to identify essential characteristics of using fractional models to compare and find equivalencies. As a team, the class would collaborate to create a short list of *We can* statements based on the qualities they identified as the best of their individual models. These *We can* statements would become the success criteria for continuing work within models in their fraction unit.

In science, we might provide learners with several samples of analyses and interpretations of data. One of the samples might "exceed expectations," another "meets expectations," and a third "needs revising." Together with the teacher, learners could discern what makes each analysis and interpretation meet the designated level of performance. The result of such an experience is the criteria for success in the form of an analytic rubric that learners will use as they engage in their own analysis and interpretations of data.

In English language arts, students may agree on characteristics of effective discussions. For example, they may generate a number of *I can* or *We can* statements based on their experiences with productive versus less productive conversations. These statements might include tracking the speaker, asking related questions, using argumentation skills, and working to reach consensus.

In history, students are often taught to analyze current events. But they may not know what it means to do so. Studying current events helps students understand the importance of people, events, and issues in the news and make connections with the past. When tasked with creating success criteria for their study of current events, students might develop a single-point rubric that includes the credibility of the source, the sector of society impact, the impact of the event (locally, nationally, or internationally), and examples of a similar event in another time period.

Co-constructing success criteria provides the most student-centered approach to establish clarity of expectations. Co-constructing is appropriate for any aspect of understanding. What often determines the success of co-constructing, no pun intended, are the samples used in the process.

YOUR TURN!

Take a look at the following continuum, starting with "teacher control" on the left and progressing to "student control" on the right. Place the different approaches to the creating and sharing of success criteria on the continuum based on the level of teacher and student control in each approach. Do your colleagues agree?

> **Approaches:** *I Can* Statements, *We Can* Statements, Single-Point Rubrics, Analytic/Holistic Rubrics, Teacher Modeling, Exemplars, and Co-Constructing Criteria for Success

Teacher Control	Student Control

Co-constructing success criteria enhances the task relevancy associated with the criteria for success. Learners are more likely to engage in a learning experience where they have input into what success looks like and how they would show what they know. Co-constructing success criteria also helps learners see the purpose and importance in learning and increases their sense of confidence that they can meet expectations. After all, they helped create them. Finally, co-constructing success criteria develops learners' capacity to independently construct success criteria to meet their goals in new contexts both in and out of school.

> Co-constructing success criteria enhances the task relevancy.

1. Do my success criteria truly represent the learning intentions for my learners?

2. Did I pick the best option for implementing success criteria based on the type of learning expected of my students?

3. Am I using success criteria to support my students taking ownership of their learning?

YOUR TURN!

Before we talk about how to set up the co-construction of success criteria, take a moment with your colleagues to identify learning intentions that you could potentially use in your upcoming lessons or unit. We will come back to this list in just a bit. For now, build the list.

LEARNING INTENTION	WHY DO YOU THINK THIS LEARNING INTENTION IS A CANDIDATE FOR CO-CONSTRUCTING SUCCESS CRITERIA?

HOW DO WE CO-CONSTRUCT SUCCESS CRITERIA?

Setting the stage for co-constructing success criteria requires that we identify the learning intention and have a clear view of the expected learning outcomes. This ensures that we select class work samples, previously made anchor charts, and targeted collections of students' individual work that will foster a high level of academic discourse and generate high expectations for success. We want to avoid "watered-down" expectations, and we can address this by being clear about the learning intention and the intentional selection of the samples.

- First select a learning intention for which you will develop success criteria.

- Make sure you are aware of the expectations provided by the standards or curriculum. This helps you formulate clarifying and probing questions when learners are analyzing samples.

- Then select class work samples, previously made anchor charts, or targeted collections of learners' individual work that will make mastery of the learning intention concrete.

- Introduce the learning intention and the task of co-constructing what success looks like or how learners will know they have met the learning intention.

- Place learners into small groups or pairs and give them copies of the class work samples, anchor charts, or their individual folders/portfolios of relevant work. The class work samples may or may not be labeled as "exceed expectations," "meets expectations," or "needs revising." This will depend on the readiness of your learners. If the samples are not labeled, the first task is for learners to identify the level of performance. Allow time for discourse and debate, moving from group to group to ask clarifying and probing questions.

- As learners begin to identify essential characteristics of each sample, provide sticky notes so they can document and organize their thinking.

- Facilitate the sharing of the success criteria by asking groups/pairs to share the criteria selected, determining commonalities across the class, and negotiating which criteria will be included in the final success criteria.

- Once success criteria have been determined, decide on the approach for showing and knowing expectations of success (e.g., *I can* statements, *We can* statements, a single-point rubric, an analytic/holistic rubric).

- Display the co-constructed *I can* statements, *We can* statements, a single-point rubric, or an analytic/holistic rubric so that the success criteria are visible as learners get started with the learning experience.

YOUR TURN!

Revisit the previous modules. Where will you and your colleagues get the tools you need (e.g., anchor charts, targeted collections of learners' individual work) to guide the co-construction? What work will need to be done over time in order to have a set of class work samples, relevant previously made anchor charts, or relevant collections of individual work (e.g., student folders/portfolios)?

LEARNING INTENTION	WHAT CHARACTERISTICS MUST THE SAMPLES HAVE?	WILL THIS COME FROM CLASS WORK SAMPLES, PREVIOUSLY MADE ANCHOR CHARTS, OR STUDENT WORK FOLDERS/PORTFOLIOS?

PATHWAY TO EQUITY: HOW DO WE GET *ALL* LEARNERS TO ENGAGE WITH CO-CONSTRUCTING SUCCESS CRITERIA?

Initial engagement in co-constructing success criteria is easy. Keeping students engaged may require a bit of guidance. Once learners co-construct the success criteria, we do not want them to never again reference those criteria. So, how will you engage your learners beyond the initial creation of success criteria? Use the space provided to map out a plan for creating and implementing co-constructing success criteria in your classroom or through your remote learning platform. Be sure to add your own ideas to our list if you feel a strategy is missing or you have one that works for you but is not included here.

> USE INTERACTIVE NOTEBOOKS.

> USE THE CO-CONSTRUCTED CRITERIA DURING THE LEARNING EXPERIENCE.

> USE THE CO-CONSTRUCTED CRITERIA FOR CLOSURE.

YOUR TURN!

We have looked at each of the different approaches to creating and sharing success criteria. Before we move forward and talk about how success criteria promote self-monitoring, self-reflection, and self-evaluation, take a moment to brainstorm how you will get your learners to not just co-construct but stay engaged with the success criteria. Record your ideas in the space provided.

Now that you have finished this module, rate yourself on each of the following success criteria using the four-item scale. Use the space provided at the end to self-reflect on your own learning. What will you do next with this information? You may not yet be at the expert level, as it takes time to integrate knowledge into practice. Use this information to identify areas of continued learning.

- I can describe ways to co-construct success criteria with students.

- I can identify the information I would need as fodder for the co-construction of success criteria.

- I can explain when the co-construction of success criteria is most likely to be effective.

- I can place the various ways for ensuring students know what success looks like along a continuum from most to least teacher control and responsibility.

MODULE 10
DIFFERENT TYPES OF SUCCESS CRITERIA FOR DIFFERENT ASPECTS OF LEARNING

Before you engage with the information in this module, rate yourself on each of the following success criteria using the four-item scale:

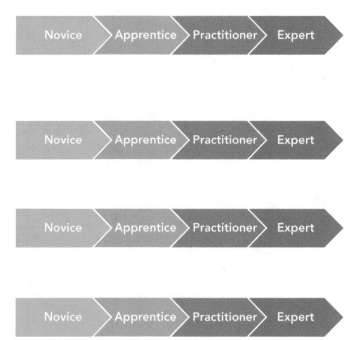

- I can describe the relationship between approaches for creating success criteria and the readiness of learners to move toward independence in learning.

  Novice Apprentice Practitioner Expert

- I can identify ways for students to demonstrate their understanding.

  Novice Apprentice Practitioner Expert

- I can use my knowledge of various ways of understanding to identify appropriate tools for developing success criteria.

  Novice Apprentice Practitioner Expert

- I can develop success criteria that focus on students' self-knowledge.

  Novice Apprentice Practitioner Expert

Modules 4–9 presented six approaches to creating and implementing success criteria from learning intentions: *I can/We can* statements, single-point rubrics, analytic/holistic rubrics, teacher modeling, exemplars, and co-constructing criteria for success. Now that you are familiar with these approaches, when might it be best to use exemplars instead of *I can* statements? How about *I can* versus *We can*? Is there a way to decide which success criteria are best implemented with analytic or holistic rubrics? The answer is that there is no one correct answer. Providing a prescriptive, fool-proof method that leads to a quick and easy way to choose the "best" approach is simply not possible. For example, if learners are using multiple representations to make sense of a contextualized problem in mathematics, teacher modeling or exemplars may be most effective in implementing the success criteria. *I can* statements may not provide clarity around what success looks like in this learning experience. Similarly, if learners are to apply their thinking about momentum and forces by designing a vehicle that would protect a raw egg in an impact collision, *I can* statements may not be as effective as a rubric in supporting transfer learning. The same reasoning applies to using text features to make meaning or comparing two historical accounts of the same event.

Instead of one right answer, the decision about how to implement success criteria requires us to closely consider the learning intentions and then leverage our professional knowledge and judgment around two main points. The following decision points guide us in deciding which approach might be best in creating and implementing success criteria:

- The readiness of learners to move toward independence in learning
- The aspect of understanding that is the focus of your learning intention

LEARNERS' READINESS TO MOVE TOWARD INDEPENDENCE IN LEARNING

One of the main decision points in deciding the best approach to creating and implementing success criteria is the readiness of our learners to operate with greater independence in a particular area.

Some *content*, *practices*, and *dispositions* will be new to learners. If this is students' initial exposure to the learning, they may require more scaffolding and support. Some learners have acquired other content, practices, and dispositions, and they may be ready to move toward deeper learning or the transfer of their learning to different contexts. The readiness of our learners to move toward greater autonomy or independence is related to where they are in this progression from initial exposure, to deeper learning, and to transfer.

Viewing the different approaches to success criteria on a continuum can help guide our decisions about how to create and implement them. When learners are moving toward deeper learning and transfer, they may be able to exercise more autonomy in engaging in success criteria. In contrast, learners early in the learning process may need more structured approaches to success criteria.

YOUR TURN!

Take another look at the following continuum, which we first described in Module 9 (see page 134). Start with "teacher control" on the left and progress to "student control" on the right. Place the different approaches to creating and implementing success criteria on the continuum based on the level of teacher and student control in each approach. Are your answers different here than in Module 9? What changed? Do your colleagues agree?

> **Approaches:** *I Can* Statements, *We Can* Statements, Single-Point Rubrics, Analytic/Holistic Rubrics, Teacher Modeling, Exemplars, and Co-Constructing Criteria for Success

Teacher Control		Student Control

As one final note, where students are in the learning process is not correlated with grade level. For example, students in calculus may be learning about integration by parts for the very first time. Thus, these learners require more structure in knowing what success looks like. In this scenario, *I can* statements and teacher modeling may work best. Kindergarteners learning about the needs of living things may be applying their learning to a school garden and can successfully co-construct success criteria.

TEACHING FOR UNDERSTANDING

So, what does it mean to understand? Wiggins and McTighe (2005) identified six aspects of student understanding. Put differently, if a student truly understands a topic, they will be able to demonstrate that understanding through the following:

1. Explanation
2. Interpretation
3. Application
4. Perspective
5. Empathy
6. Self-knowledge

These six aspects of understanding also help us with knowing and showing success. Let's look at each of these aspects and examples of learning intentions that exemplify each aspect of understanding.

ASPECT OF UNDERSTANDING	MATHEMATICS LEARNING INTENTIONS	SCIENCE LEARNING INTENTIONS	ENGLISH LANGUAGE ARTS LEARNING INTENTIONS	HISTORY/ SOCIAL STUDIES LEARNING INTENTIONS
Explanation: Learners provide a thorough and justifiable account of phenomena, content, and data.	*Middle School:* We are learning about the relationships between the volume of a prism and a pyramid and between the volume of a cylinder and a cone.	*High School:* We are learning about the relationship between catalysts and rates of reactions.	*Elementary School:* We are learning to identify the points of view of different characters.	*Elementary School:* We are learning about food production and consumption now and long ago.
Interpretation: Learners offer translations, make content accessible through multiple representations and models, and add personal perspective.	*Elementary School:* I am learning about the core of a repeating pattern and translating it using multiple types of materials, images, and actions.	*High School:* I am learning about the process for analyzing motion sensor data generated from a laboratory on distance, velocity, and acceleration.	*Elementary School:* We are learning to use illustrations and words to understand characters, settings, and plots.	*Middle School:* We are learning about the historic influence of tea.
Application: Learners use what they know and can do in a different context or scenario.	*High School:* I am learning how a three-act task can represent a real-life situation exemplifying an inverse function.	*Middle School:* I am learning how water filtration systems can be used to eliminate pollutants in drinking water.	*Middle School:* I am learning to identify an author's point of view in different texts on the same topic.	*High School:* I am learning to apply my knowledge of economic systems to various countries across time.
Perspective: Learners take diverse points of view regarding the content, confronting alternative theories or explanations.	*Elementary School:* We are learning about exclusive and inclusive definitions of a trapezoid and demonstrating how the classification hierarchy of polygons is affected by each.	*High School:* We are learning about deforestation from the perspective of different regions and countries.	*High School:* We are applying a feminist lens to our literacy critiques.	*Elementary School:* We are learning about competing claims for control of land.
Empathy: Learners see the world through someone else's point of view and openly embrace ideas, experiences, and perspectives of their peers.	*High School:* I am learning about the ways statisticians strategically use measures of center and population sampling to convince consumers.	*Elementary School:* I am learning that there are different perspectives on whether we should recycle.	*Elementary School:* We are writing narratives from the perspective of Auggie (from the book *Wonder*).	*Middle School:* We are studying the lives of Black Americans who gained freedom in the North and founded schools and churches to advance their rights and communities.

CONTINUED

ASPECT OF UNDERSTANDING	MATHEMATICS LEARNING INTENTIONS	SCIENCE LEARNING INTENTIONS	ENGLISH LANGUAGE ARTS LEARNING INTENTIONS	HISTORY/ SOCIAL STUDIES LEARNING INTENTIONS
Self-Knowledge: Learners are aware of their own perspectives, self-question their own understanding, and are self-reflective.	*Middle School:* I am learning the value of precise units, labels, calculations, and mathematical language.	*Elementary School:* I am learning about human impact on the environment.	*High School:* I am writing a first-person narrative in response to the question: *Who am I?*	*Elementary School:* I am learning about fair play and good sportsmanship.

 Available for download at **resources.corwin.com/successcriteriaplaybook**

The key message here is that the aspect of understanding should be considered in deciding which approach to success criteria we should use. For example, if we are after self-knowledge, the use of a single-point rubric or co-constructed success criteria may be a great starting point. When the aspect of understanding is interpretation, teacher modeling or an exemplar might be a great starting point.

1. Do my success criteria truly represent the learning intentions for my learners?

2. Did I pick the best option for implementing success criteria based on the type of learning expected of my students?

3. Am I using success criteria to support my students taking ownership of their learning?

YOUR TURN!

Returning to the different ways of creating and implementing success criteria, which aspects of understanding do you believe best align with the different criteria for success? When your learning intention is centered around a specific aspect of understanding, which format for success criteria would make clear what this type of understanding looks like and sounds like upon mastery? *Keep in mind, there can be multiple success criteria options for each aspect of understanding* (e.g., rubrics work for more than one aspect of understanding). Use your initial understandings of the ways of implementing success criteria and the aspects of understanding as well as your experiences to make connections.

This task is best done in conversation with colleagues so that you can discuss why you believe certain types of success criteria are best aligned with certain aspects of understanding. Sharing and discussing different perspectives will help us stay focused on the purpose of creating and implementing success criteria: *to better connect our learners to a shared understanding of what success looks like for any given process, task, or product.*

APPROACHES TO SUCCESS CRITERIA	ASPECTS OF UNDERSTANDING
I Can Statements	
We Can Statements	
Single-Point Rubrics	
Analytic/Holistic Rubrics	
Teacher Modeling	
Exemplars	
Co-Constructing Criteria for Success	

While we always want our learners to hold a shared understanding of what success looks like, each of the aspects of understanding calls for a different approach to sharing criteria for success. The content and format of success criteria change depending on and in alignment with the learning intentions.

> The content and format of success criteria change depending on and in alignment with the learning intentions.

YOUR TURN! ✏️

Return to your work in Module 1, specifically page 20. Take a moment and review your work before moving forward with this exercise. Consider the *content*, *practices*, and *dispositions* that would indicate that a learner have mastered the learning intention. Let's add to this work by deciding which way of creating and implementing success criteria fits best. If you and your colleagues would like to consider a different or upcoming topic, that is even better!

	TOPIC	ASPECT OF UNDERSTANDING	WAYS OF KNOWING AND SHOWING SUCCESS CRITERIA
What is the learning intention?			
What would learners say and do if they have mastered the learning intention? (content, practices, and dispositions)	1. 2. 3. 4. 5.		

In Module 11, we will explore not only how to show success criteria to our learners but also how to engage them in making sense of and using the success criteria to self-monitor, self-reflect, and self-evaluate.

Now that you have finished this module, rate yourself on each of the following success criteria using the four-item scale. Use the space provided at the end to self-reflect on your own learning. What will you do next with this information? You may not yet be at the expert level, as it takes time to integrate knowledge into practice. Use this information to identify areas of continued learning.

- I can describe the relationship between approaches for creating success criteria and the readiness of learners to move toward independence in learning.

| Novice | Apprentice | Practitioner | Expert |

- I can identify ways for students to demonstrate their understanding.

| Novice | Apprentice | Practitioner | Expert |

- I can use my knowledge of various ways of understanding to identify appropriate tools for developing success criteria.

| Novice | Apprentice | Practitioner | Expert |

- I can develop success criteria that focus on students' self-knowledge.

| Novice | Apprentice | Practitioner | Expert |

NOTES ✏️

_____

_____

_____

_____

_____

_____

_____

_____

_____

_____

_____

_____

_____

_____

_____

_____

_____

_____

_____

_____

_____

_____

_____

PART 3

MODULE 11
HOW DO WE USE SUCCESS CRITERIA TO FOSTER META-COGNITION?

Before you engage with the information in this module, rate yourself on each of the following success criteria using the four-item scale:

- I can describe the relationship between approaches for creating success criteria and the readiness of learners to move toward independence in learning.

- I can identify ways for students to demonstrate their understanding.

- I can describe the characteristics of assessment-capable visible learners.

- I can identify ways that success criteria can contribute to the development of assessment-capable learners, especially students who self-monitor, self-reflect, and self-evaluate.

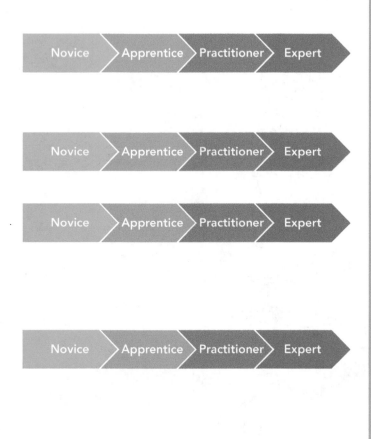

High-quality success criteria not only make the learning intention visible; success criteria also help define the learning intention. The visibility of and definitions within learning intentions and success criteria lay the foundation for *all* learners to take greater ownership of their own learning journey. Success criteria support **all students** as they develop the characteristics of assessment-capable visible learners (Frey, Hattie, & Fisher, 2018).

High-quality success criteria not only make the learning intention visible; success criteria also help define the learning intention.

ASSESSMENT-CAPABLE VISIBLE LEARNERS

- Know their current level of understanding.
- Know where they are going next and are ready to take on the challenge.
- Select the best tools or strategies to move their learning forward.
- Recognize that mistakes are opportunities for learning and seek feedback.
- Monitor their progress and make adjustments in the learning when needed.
- Recognize when they have met the learning intentions and support their peers.

Each of these six characteristics requires learners to self-monitor, self-reflect, and self-evaluate. High-quality success criteria provide the clarity necessary for learners to self-monitor, self-reflect, and self-evaluate. Our role as teachers is to foster these three meta-cognitive strategies in our students by explicitly connecting the success criteria with their learning.

High-quality success criteria provide the clarity necessary for learners to self-monitor, self-reflect, and self-evaluate.

YOUR TURN!

With your colleagues, engage in a needs assessment around the three meta-cognitive strategies we just described. Where do you think your learners are in their journey toward self-monitoring, self-reflection, and self-evaluation?

META-COGNITIVE STRATEGY	WHERE ARE YOUR LEARNERS?	EXPLAIN WHY YOU BELIEVE THIS IS WHERE THEY ARE IN THEIR JOURNEY. WHAT EVIDENCE ARE YOU USING TO MAKE THAT ASSESSMENT?
Self-Monitoring	Not Yet Getting There There	
Self-Reflection	Not Yet Getting There There	
Self-Evaluation	Not Yet Getting There There	

SELF-MONITORING WITH SUCCESS CRITERIA

When students effectively self-monitor their learning, they keep a mental or physical record of the journey and use that record to make adjustments when necessary. This includes the time they are spending or should spend on specific content, practices, and dispositions. For example, learners may self-monitor the amount of effort and thinking they are putting into developing a conceptual model of division, discerning between an angiosperm and gymnosperm, identifying the ways in which the author's craft impacts a message, or determining how much studying to do. They *could* then use that information to make decisions about how to allocate time and direct their thinking during centers or stations. Some learners may need support with self-monitoring. Learners who are still developing this meta-cognitive strategy might find it challenging to monitor their learning time during centers and stations; for example, they may not recognize that time is needed for either modeling division or discerning angiosperms and gymnosperms.

Effective self-monitors also keep a close watch on the situational conditions of their learning, including what they are thinking about, how they are feeling toward the learning, and what they are doing to move their learning forward. This helps them identify when things are going well and when things are not going so well. If they encounter a challenge with their mental model of division, they recognize the incongruency in their thinking. On the other hand, learners may not recognize that their sorting of angiosperms and gymnosperms has created an incongruency in their conceptual understanding, thus indicating the need for more scaffolding and support from us.

High-quality success criteria foster, nurture, and sustain self-monitoring by defining the learning intention and making it visible to teachers and learners. We can use success criteria to help develop self-monitoring. Instead of simply expecting learners to self-monitor, we can scaffold this meta-cognitive skill by providing structures that require learners to self-monitor. Then, over time, we slowly remove those structures as learners begin to self-monitor without prompting from us.

> Instead of simply expecting learners to self-monitor, we can scaffold this meta-cognitive skill by providing structures that require learners to self-monitor.

YOUR TURN!

At the end of Modules 4–9, we looked at different ways to engage learners in each type of success criteria. Revisit those ideas. Then, use those ideas to develop your own scaffolded approach to developing self-monitoring in your learners. Use the space provided to map out this approach. An example is provided for you.

Highly Scaffolded   Less Scaffolded   Independent Self-Monitoring

Turn and talk about *I can* or *We can* statements with a partner at the start of the lesson.

SELF-REFLECTION WITH SUCCESS CRITERIA

Self-monitoring is one thing. How we use the mental or physical record of the journey is something different. Self-reflection engages learners in thinking about the mental or physical record to make meaning of their time, effort, and situational conditions. In other words, self-monitoring is recognizing; self-reflection is making sense of it. For learners, self-reflection builds on self-monitoring by describing the record of the journey based on where the learning is going, how it is going, and where to go next in the learning. Learners who are good at self-reflection would not only recognize a challenge with their mental model of division, but they would also think about that challenge and the implications for where they go next in their learning journey. Likewise, effective self-monitors would recognize that their sorting of angiosperms and gymnosperms has created an incongruency in their conceptual understanding. Good self-reflectors would consider what this means for their own learning. Students who are focused on the author's craft (such as narration, genre choices, and literary devices) notice the moves of the authors they study and incorporate those moves into their writing. Similarly, students who note that there are things they need to study

have likely engaged in some reflection about their performance in order to allocate resources to areas needing attention.

> Self-monitoring is recognizing; self-reflection is making sense of it.

Effective self-reflection requires that learners place the mental or physical record of the learning journey within the context of three key reflective questions:

1. Where am I going in this learning journey?

2. How is it going for me?

3. Where do I go next in my learning journey?

How learners mentally respond to these questions is the difference between learners who make adjustments to their learning and continue to move forward and learners who immediately raise their hand and profess that they "don't get it."

High-quality success criteria foster, nurture, and sustain self-reflection by defining the learning intention and making it visible to teachers and learners. We can also use success criteria to support the development of this meta-cognitive strategy. Much like self-monitoring, we can scaffold learners' thinking about their learning.

YOUR TURN!

Revisit the ideas for engaging learners in success criteria found at the end of Modules 4–9. This time, use those ideas to develop your own scaffolded approach to fostering self-reflection in your learners. Use the space provided to map out this approach. An example is provided for you.

Highly Scaffolded   Less Scaffolded   Independent Self-Monitoring

A learner gets stuck and asks herself, *What have I done so far? What is not making sense to me? What questions do I have? What resources can I use to help me get unstuck?*

SELF-EVALUATION WITH SUCCESS CRITERIA

To self-evaluate, learners must mentally or physically keep a record of the learning journey, reflect or think about that record, and then view it next to standards of comparison to determine where they stand relative to a specific target. In our classrooms, the target is the learning intention and the standards of comparison are the success criteria. With the development of a conceptual model for division, learners would need to recognize the challenge relative to their initial understanding, reflect on the nature of that challenge, and then evaluate if their response to that challenge moved them closer to the target. If learners were monitoring their learning and made an adjustment, self-evaluation would allow them to see if they had resolved the challenge or if they needed to seek additional support and feedback from their peers or the teacher. Self-evaluation does not always come at the end of learning or the completion of a task; learners can engage in self-evaluation during learning or mid-task in order to make adjustments based on the shared vision for success.

Let's look closer at the example of discerning angiosperms and gymnosperms. During a sorting task, an effective self-monitor recognizes the inconsistency in his work (e.g., an image of a flower is in both the angiosperm and gymnosperm columns). Through self-reflection, this student considers that the flowers should be in the same column and he quickly moves one image so that both are in the angiosperm column. He then checks the success criteria and self-evaluates. The student notices that one of the success criteria states, *I can explain the differences between angiosperms and gymnosperms.* Through self-evaluation, this learner knows that is not the case

and immediately seeks additional support (e.g., by looking in his interactive notebook, discussing the sorting task with a peer, and/or seeking additional feedback from the teacher).

From the learner's perspective

- self-evaluation is comparing my work to the success criteria,
- self-reflection is reflecting on whether what I'm doing or not doing is helping me get there.

This happens with younger students as well. For example, a student who notices that she is not understanding what she is reading has engaged in monitoring. That's important but not sufficient. To unlock the meaning of the text, the student would need to reflect on what got in the way. Perhaps it was vocabulary. But maybe it was attention. Or maybe it was the structure or length of the sentences. Students who have strong self-reflection skills in English language arts notice when meaning is lost and they have tools to regain comprehension. To solidify the experience, the student would evaluate whether the change or tool made a difference. If the student said to herself, "I was distracted and now I'm more focused and it's making sense to me," then this learner has demonstrated all three meta-cognitive skills. Of course, there are times when the reflection reveals a need for more learning and students turn to their peers or teachers for support.

High-quality success criteria foster, nurture, and sustain self-evaluation by defining the learning intention and making it visible to teachers and learners. The development of self-evaluation is supported through success criteria. But like the other two meta-cognitive strategies, this requires intentional scaffolding for our learners.

YOUR TURN!

Revisit the ideas for engaging learners in success criteria found at the end of Modules 4–9 one last time. Now use those ideas to develop your own scaffolded approach to developing self-evaluation. Use the space provided to map out this approach. As in the earlier Your Turn! exercises, we provide an example.

Highly Scaffolded   Less Scaffolded   Independent Self-Monitoring

Gather students mid-lesson and have them talk in pairs about the guiding questions that refer to the relationship between the rubric and their work. Have them write down their next steps. Then release students to work again with new or renewed direction for next steps.

FROM *I CAN* TO *CAN I?*

With high-quality success criteria, we can transition any criterion into an opportunity for self-monitoring, self-reflection, or self-evaluation. Consider the following success criteria from earlier in this module.

- I can model my thinking about dividing numbers.
- I can compare and contrast angiosperms and gymnosperms.
- I can identify the impact of the author's craft on my understanding of the text.
- I can analyze my work to identify areas that I need to study.

One way to guide learners to monitor their learning, reflect on their thinking, and evaluate their progress is to transform the *I can* statements into *Can I?* questions.

This task is further enriched when learners are expected to not only answer the question with

- Can I model my thinking about dividing numbers?
- Can I compare and contrast angiosperms and gymnosperms?
- Can I identify the impact of the author's craft on my understanding of the text?
- Can I analyze my work to identify areas that I need to study?

a yes or no response but also provide evidence to support their responses. For example, if the answer to the question *Can I model my thinking about dividing numbers?* is no, we can engage in reflective dialogue with the learner to understand why. We might ask, *Why can't you model your thinking? What do you need to be able to model your thinking?*

Whether we are using *I can* statements, *We can* statements, or any other approach to creating and implementing success criteria, turning them into questions supports self-monitoring, self-reflection, and self-evaluation.

YOUR TURN! ✏️

We have worked to develop many success criteria over the course of this playbook. Using success criteria that you and your colleagues developed across Modules 4–9, transform them into self-monitoring, self-reflection, and self-evaluation questions. Then, map out a plan to use these questions in an upcoming learning experience or series of lessons. Refer to the above examples (i.e., *I can* to *Can I?*) to get started.

Now that you have finished this module, rate yourself on each of the following success criteria using the four-item scale. Use the space provided at the end to self-reflect on your own learning. What will you do next with this information? You may not yet be at the expert level, as it takes time to integrate knowledge into practice. Use this information to identify areas of continued learning.

- I can describe the relationship between approaches for creating success criteria and the readiness of learners to move toward independence in learning.

- I can identify ways for students to demonstrate their understanding.

- I can describe the characteristics of assessment-capable visible learners.

- I can identify ways that success criteria can contribute to the development of assessment-capable learners, especially students who self-monitor, self-reflect, and self-evaluate.

MODULE 12
HOW DO SUCCESS CRITERIA SUPPORT DELIBERATE PRACTICE AND TRANSFER OF LEARNING?

Before you engage with the information in this module, rate yourself on each of the following success criteria using the four-item scale:

- I can compare naïve and deliberate practice.

- I can describe the differences between acquisition, fluency, maintenance, and transfer.

- I can describe the aspects of deliberate practice.

- I can use *I can* statements to help students self-monitor, self-reflect, and self-evaluate.

We are all familiar with the phrase "practice makes perfect." As it turns out, this statement is not entirely true. Not all practice makes perfect, nor is all practice effective at moving learning forward. The more correct phrasing would be "practice makes permanent." As teachers, our attention immediately turns to the word *permanent*. There are certain pieces of information, processes, and dispositions that we want permanently encoded into our learners' brains, and then there are things we do not want permanently etched into their brains. However, we know that learners must practice to progress in their learning. So, what we really want to know is what type of practice best supports learners as they progress toward the learning intentions? Furthermore, what does this have to do with success criteria?

YOUR TURN!

Take a moment to make a list of all the different ways you and your colleagues get learners to practice. Jot down specific ways you offer learners opportunities to practice *content*, *practices*, and *dispositions*. We will come back to this list later in this module. For now, just create the list.

TWO DIFFERENT WAYS TO PRACTICE

There are two different kinds of practice: naïve practice and deliberate practice (Ericsson, 2008; Ericsson & Pool, 2016). Naïve practice is practice that simply accumulates experience. This type of practice is typically without purpose in that learners are simply going through the motions (Ericsson, Krampe, & Tesch-Romer, 1993). In mathematics, an example of naïve practice would be learners playing mathematics games simply because that was the next task in their rotation or on the agenda. Another example would be learners simply solving the same type of problem over and over again because that was the assignment. For science, naïve practice would be learners repeatedly going over the parts of the water cycle, reviewing the steps in mitosis and meiosis, or calculating the formula weight of different substances. Another example of naïve practice is writing a word 10 times, or 100 times for that matter, thinking that it improves spelling. Similarly, memorizing dates and facts using flash cards is not likely to ensure deep understanding of history.

In deliberate practice, learners pinpoint a particular piece of content, a practice, or a disposition that they want to improve on. Then, learners focus their time on specifically improving in that particular content, practice, or disposition until it can be integrated into other learning. Deliberate practice is a mindful and structured way of learning by targeting areas needing improvement (Ericsson et al., 1993).

In mathematics, a learner may recognize that he struggles with adding two-digit numbers that sum to greater than 100. Deliberate practice could still involve having learners play a game, but the game should be chosen intentionally to target this area of need and should focus on strategies to combine two-digit numbers. If a learner found multistep contextualized problems confusing, deliberate practice would involve acting out, sketching, or visualizing and talking out similar problems to make sense of them but not worry about actually solving them yet; thus, the learning focuses on the targeted area of need in a structured way.

In science, a learner may recognize that she has considerable difficulty in metric conversions, especially in units of energy, force, and momentum. For spelling, deliberate practice might involve repeated spelling "tests" in which the learner analyzes the location in the word where the error occurred and then focuses his learning on that spelling pattern, generalizing to other words with a similar pattern (to note, we recognize that not all words used in language work this way).

Deliberate practice focuses on a particular skill, and learners strive to work out all of the issues that come up with this skill. If a learner encountered problems understanding the relationship between energy transfer in changing states of matter, he would engage in practice sessions that targeted this concept and his understanding of the concept. If a learner encountered challenges remembering the differences between Athens and Sparta (or the French, Russian, American, and Glorious Revolutions), practice sessions would need to help her gain clarity on this concept.

> Deliberate practice focuses on a particular skill, and learners strive to work out all of the issues that come up with this skill.

YOUR TURN!

Return now to your list of the different ways you and your colleagues get learners to practice (page 165). Knowing what you know now, which items on the list would be classified as naïve practice and which items on the list are deliberate practice? Don't worry about the number of items for each practice type. We will talk about that next. For now, put an N by those you classify as naïve practice and a D by those you classify as deliberate practice.

WHICH ONE IS BETTER?

Whether naïve or deliberate practice is best depends on the learners and where they are in the learning process. Let's start with the learning process (Figure 12.1) and then sort out whether naïve or deliberate practice is best.

Learners begin with the acquisition of new *content*, *skills*, *practices*, and *dispositions* (e.g., identifying algebraic properties, understanding enthalpy and thermodynamics, forming letters, constructing viable arguments, noticing dialogue, engaging in critical thinking, developing and using models, examining bias, communicating technical information). With practice, they

develop fluency in that content, with those practices, and in the application of dispositions. The step from acquisition to fluency is facilitated through deliberate practice. Deliberate practice leads to mastery and then to what is referred to as automaticity (Ericsson & Pool, 2016). This is when learners fully integrate the learning into their thinking. In mathematics, learners acquire new learning about equivalent fractions and decimals, especially benchmark numbers. In science, learners acquire new learning around Coulomb's law and electrostatic forces. In English language arts, students learn about writing opinions and arguments with reasons and evidence. In social studies, students learn to distinguish fact from opinion and the role of

FIGURE 12.1 **The Process for Learning Fluency and Mastery**

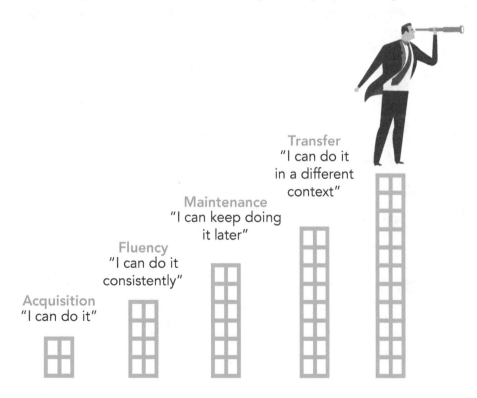

Transfer
"I can do it in a different context"

Maintenance
"I can keep doing it later"

Fluency
"I can do it consistently"

Acquisition
"I can do it"

primary source documents in telling a story. To develop fluency in this knowledge, including practices, students will need to engage in deliberate practice that pinpoints where they need to improve in their learning and devote focused practice time to that specific area needing improvement.

> Deliberate practice leads to mastery and then to what is referred to as automaticity.

Yet we cannot stop at fluency. Over time, learners need to engage in maintenance. This requires learners to retrieve the content, practices, and dispositions to maintain their level of fluency. In the end, this knowledge becomes generalizable or transferrable to new contexts. Maintenance and transfer are facilitated through naïve practice. For mathematics, this occurs when learners recall familiar or benchmark equivalencies through naïve practice. With regard to Coulomb's law, learners would need to engage in naïve practice over time to maintain fluency and support transfer. The same happens with learning to write and learning how various events in history are related to one another in time. To support transfer with naïve practice, timing the practice to when the content, practice, and disposition may be helpful.

> We cannot stop at fluency. Over time, learners need to engage in maintenance.

To be clear, deliberate practice is the type of practice that best supports learners as they progress toward the learning intentions. Deliberate practice moves learners to mastery of *content*, *skills*, *practices*, and *dispositions*. However, naïve practice has its place in our classrooms. The success criteria determine the place for both types of practice.

YOUR TURN!

Let's return to a list of success criteria you have created in this playbook. Pull any of the criteria created from Modules 3–8. List the criteria and their associated learning intention in the following chart. Then, in the columns to the right, develop a plan for how you will engage learners in deliberate practice and where you will offer them opportunities for naïve practice. Remember, deliberate practice pinpoints areas needing improvement. That is the purpose of the column that asks how learners will know they need to deliberately practice. Several examples are provided for you.

LEARNING INTENTION	SUCCESS CRITERIA	WAYS TO DELIBERATELY PRACTICE	HOW WILL LEARNERS KNOW THEY NEED TO DELIBERATELY PRACTICE?	OPPORTUNITIES FOR NAÏVE PRACTICE
I am learning that the areas of polygons can be composed by and decomposed into other familiar polygons.	• I can use the area of a rectangle to find the area of any triangle. • I can compose any polygon into rectangles to find its area. • I can decompose any polygon into triangles to find its area. • I can explain how to visualize any polygon as composed of other familiar shapes to find its area.	• Use manipulatives, sketches, folding, and visualizing to compose and decompose polygons. • Have students find in their environment or create mystery shapes and find their areas.	• Hold conferences with students during problem solving. • Discuss explanations and reflections within problem-solving tasks. • Conduct formative assessments, such as exit tasks and hinge questions (Fennell et al., 2017).	• Sketch quick images of composed and decomposed polygons. • Find areas of mystery shapes as weekly may-do tasks.
I am learning about the law of conservation of mass in isolated systems.	• I can balance a simple chemical reaction. • I can balance a complex reaction. • I can predict the products of a chemical reaction.	• Offer different homework assignments based on areas needing improvement; use small-group instruction; use a learning contract.	• Use evidence from entrance and exit tickets. • Listen to student questions and discussions.	• Continue to put questions relating to this topic on upcoming entrance tickets, exit tickets, and other assessments.
I am learning 15 new sight words.	• I can identify words from our word wall when I am reading.	• Read vocabulary-controlled and decodable texts.	• During small-group reading instruction, notice which words students have mastered and which require additional instruction and/or practice.	• Use a flashcard app to practice words. • Read words from the word wall chorally as a class. • Send lists of sight words home with parents to practice.
We are learning about the influence of China and Korea on ancient Japan.	• I can describe the ways that China and Korea impacted Japan. • I can identify intellectual, linguistic, religious, and philosophical impacts from China and Korea on Japan.	• Read from a variety of sources on the subject based on areas of need. • Watch videos on the learning management system (LMS) that provide needed information based on the practice test.	• Use a formative practice test to identify areas of strength and need. • Ask students to analyze their results and develop study plans.	• Create a graphic organizer or note page. • Take the quizzes in the LMS that provide corrective feedback and opportunities to retake them.

CONTINUED

Module 12: How Do Success Criteria Support Deliberate Practice and Transfer of Learning?

169

LEARNING INTENTION	SUCCESS CRITERIA	WAYS TO DELIBERATELY PRACTICE	HOW WILL LEARNERS KNOW THEY NEED TO DELIBERATELY PRACTICE?	OPPORTUNITIES FOR NAÏVE PRACTICE

online resources

THE ROLE OF SUCCESS CRITERIA

Ericsson and Pool (2016) describe the following process for engaging in deliberate practice:

1. Define the goal.
2. Establish the elements of success for that goal.
3. Determine where there is a need for improvement or growth.
4. Engage in a focused and planned practice session.
5. Receive feedback on the practice session.
6. Reflect on the improvement and growth after each practice session.
7. Plan the next practice session.

This process continues until the learner has developed fluency in the particular area of improvement or growth. At this point in the playbook, you can see the connection between learning intentions, success criteria, and deliberate practice. Plus, deliberate practice is best supported with a coach. The coach is you—the teacher. Thus, the *We can* aspect of success criteria is all the more important.

Whether *I can/We can* statements, single-point rubrics, analytic/holistic rubrics, modeling, exemplars, or co-constructed success criteria are used, these powerful components of a learning intention also point to where learners may need deliberate practice.

YOUR TURN!

So that we develop fluency with the characteristics of success criteria, see if you can recall them from earlier modules. If you need additional support, they are found at the beginning of Module 1 (page 16).

When given success criteria that are actionable and represent components of the learning intention, our learners can locate very specific aspects of the learning where they can improve. Plus, if we integrate the strategies for self-monitoring, self-reflection, and self-evaluation from Module 11, we can partner with learners and let them set their own practice goals based on feedback around the success criteria. And, as we have emphasized throughout this entire playbook, we have many different ways for creating and implementing success criteria. In addition, when learning intentions are broken down into several success criteria, or what Ericsson and Pool (2016) call smaller data points, learners will see progress sooner than later, develop confidence and efficacy, and be motivated to continue making progress toward the learning intentions.

> We can partner with learners and let them set their own practice goals based on feedback around the success criteria. And, as we have emphasized throughout this entire playbook, we have many different ways for creating and implementing success criteria.

YOUR TURN!

We pointed out earlier that deliberate practice is best supported with a coach. In our classrooms, the learners' coach could be us or it could also be their peers. Take a moment to develop a plan for learners to receive both peer feedback and coaching from you and/or their peers on the success criteria you have listed in the prior Your Turn! exercise.

As we move to the next module, notice that feedback is an essential part of deliberate practice. Module 13 takes an in-depth look at feedback and the role of deliberate practice and success criteria in giving and receiving feedback.

Now that you have finished this module, rate yourself on each of the following success criteria using the four-item scale. Use the space provided at the end to self-reflect on your own learning. What will you do next with this information? You may not yet be at the expert level, as it takes time to integrate knowledge into practice. Use this information to identify areas of continued learning.

- I can compare naïve and deliberate practice.

| Novice | Apprentice | Practitioner | Expert |

- I can describe the differences between acquisition, fluency, maintenance, and transfer.

| Novice | Apprentice | Practitioner | Expert |

- I can describe the aspects of deliberate practice.

| Novice | Apprentice | Practitioner | Expert |

- I can use *I can* statements to help students self-monitor, self-reflect, and self-evaluate.

| Novice | Apprentice | Practitioner | Expert |

NOTES

_____

_____

_____

_____

_____

_____

_____

_____

_____

_____

_____

_____

_____

_____

_____

_____

_____

_____

_____

_____

_____

_____

_____

_____

MODULE 13
WHAT IS THE RELATIONSHIP BETWEEN SUCCESS CRITERIA AND FEEDBACK?

Before you engage with the information in this module, rate yourself on each of the following success criteria using the four-item scale:

- I can compare teacher feedback, student feedback, and self-feedback.

- I can describe the role of success criteria in structuring feedback.

- I can describe features of feedback that impact learning.

- I can distinguish between more and less effective feedback.

Let's start with a definition of feedback. By definition, *feedback* is the exchange of evaluative or corrective information about an action, event, or process and is the basis for improvement (Merriam-Webster, 1999). This exchange of information as the basis for improvement is our focus in this module. Feedback only supports improvement when the information is received and effectively integrated into the learning process. There is a difference in impact between feedback that is sent and feedback that is received. To increase the likelihood that feedback is received and has an impact on increasing

learning, feedback must address three very important questions for both the teacher and the learners (Hattie, 2012):

1. Where are we going?
2. How are we going?
3. Where do we go next?

YOUR TURN!

Take a moment to brainstorm the relationship between high-quality success criteria and the capacity for both the teacher and the learners to respond to these questions. In other words, predict where we are going in this module. What is the relationship between feedback and success criteria?

FEEDBACK QUESTIONS	RELATIONSHIP TO SUCCESS CRITERIA
Where are we going?	
How are we going?	
Where do we go next?	

DECIDING WHAT FEEDBACK TO GIVE AND RECEIVE

Feedback has a powerful impact on learning. For feedback to work, teachers have to understand the following:

- Learners' expected level of performance
- Learners' current level of performance
- Actions teachers can take to close the gap

Feedback is designed to close the gap between learners' current location in the learning progression and the next level or place in the progression, which we call the success criteria (Figure 13.1). With this information, learners can begin to support their self-monitoring, self-reflection, and self-evaluation of their learning to meet the learning intention.

FIGURE 13.1 **Feedback and Success Criteria**

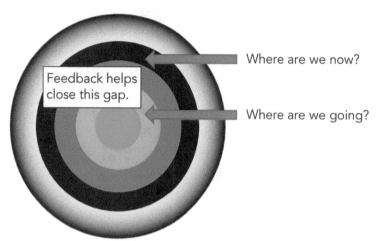

Where are we now?

Where are we going?

Feedback helps close this gap.

- The feedback given and received should specifically target what learners are expected to say and do to demonstrate that they have met the learning intention.

- Feedback should be customized based on what students are currently able to say and do and on what actions would be helpful in closing the gap.

- Feedback provides guidance about the impact of deliberate practice and whether learners have moved forward in their learning.

The last bullet highlights one of the many benefits of deliberate practice: feedback provides guidance about the impact of deliberate practice and whether learners have moved forward in their learning. In Module 12, we explored the value of deliberate practice. To reiterate the connection, success criteria guide our decisions about what specific *content*, *practices*, and *dispositions* need deliberate practice. So, feedback provides guidance, but it's only when the feedback is received that it works. Giving feedback is different from receiving feedback.

YOUR TURN!

Let's return to the set of success criteria from Module 4. They are provided below. For feedback to be effective, the information must focus on the learners' current level of performance, the expected level of performance, and how to close the gap. What, specifically, should the feedback focus on in the following situations?

LEARNING INTENTIONS	EXAMPLES OF SUCCESS CRITERIA	FOCUS OF THE FEEDBACK
Mathematics		
We are learning to select fluent subtraction strategies.	• We can select an efficient and appropriate subtraction strategy based on the numbers and situation. • We can defend our reasoning to our peers and understand their reasoning too. • We can apply the strategy to find an accurate solution.	
We are learning to estimate length measurements.	• We can estimate length using our personal benchmarks for centimeters, meters, and kilometers. • We can estimate length using a visual referent for comparison. • We can describe our estimates using mathematical language: *about, close to, more than, less than, between.* • We can evaluate the reasonableness of a peer's solution based on our estimates.	
I am learning about the role of irrational numbers within the number system.	• I can explain the difference between a rational and an irrational number. • I can collaborate to name irrational numbers and estimate their approximate locations on a number line using rational numbers as benchmarks.	
Science		
I am learning about the law of conservation of mass in isolated systems.	• I can balance a simple chemical reaction. • I can balance a complex reaction. • I can predict the products of a chemical reaction.	

CONTINUED

CONTINUED

LEARNING INTENTIONS	EXAMPLES OF SUCCESS CRITERIA	FOCUS OF THE FEEDBACK
We are learning about the role of energy transfer in the rock cycle.	• We can identify each of the three types of rocks. • We can describe how their properties provide evidence of how they were formed.	
I am learning about the impact of humans on the environment.	• I can give examples of how humans impact the environment. • I can describe how these actions impact specific parts of the ecosystem. • I can collaboratively propose possible solutions that will lessen that impact.	
I am learning about energy transfer in matter.	• I can describe how matter changes from one form to another.	
English Language Arts		
I am learning to analyze the impact of word choice on tone.	• I can describe the difference between mood and tone. • I can identify words that might set the tone. • I can analyze the words and identify the tone.	
I am learning about informational text structures.	• I can use signal words to identify the structure of a text. • I can explain the characteristics of common types of text structures. • I can use my knowledge about text structure to organize my notes.	
Social Studies		
We are learning about the contributions of Muslim scholars and their impact on later civilizations.	• We can describe contributions from Muslim scholars in the areas of science and medicine. • We can describe contributions from Muslim scholars in the areas of philosophy, art, and literature. • We can describe contributions from Muslim scholars in the area of mathematics.	

FEATURES OF EFFECTIVE FEEDBACK

The following are features of effective feedback.

1. *Focus on learning, not the individual.* Effective feedback should focus on the learning and not the individual participating in the learning. Here's an example: "My explanation of energy transfer in the water cycle needs improving, not me as a person. My solution to the mathematics problem is wrong, but I am not a wrong person. My writing is not clear, but I am not a bad writer. My understanding of the historical timeline is fuzzy, but I am not stupid."

2. *Feedback needs to be specific to the learner and delivered when and where it can best benefit the learner.*

There are different strategies for giving feedback to and receiving feedback from our learners. To increase the chances that this feedback will be received and therefore support the learning, feedback should vary in terms of timing, amount, mode, and audience (see Brookhart, 2008). Let's look a bit closer at the variables of time, amount, mode, and audience.

> Feedback should vary in terms of timing, amount, mode, and audience.

YOUR TURN!

Take a look at the variables of *timing*, *amount*, *mode*, and *audience* in the following chart. With your colleagues, do the following:

- Talk through each of these variables and how this would look in *your* classrooms.
- Ask yourselves if you missed any of the things to consider for each variable.
- Discuss how you can engage learners in this process. Are there ways to pull ideas from Module 11 on fostering meta-cognition? Take a moment to revisit those ideas.

When you intentionally work to include peer-to-peer feedback, you take advantage of the value in dialogue between peers and scaffold the development of self-monitoring, self-reflection, and self-evaluation.

FEEDBACK STRATEGIES CAN VARY IN TERMS OF . . .	IN THESE WAYS . . .	EXAMPLES AND THINGS TO CONSIDER	HOW CAN WE INCORPORATE PEER-TO-PEER FEEDBACK?
Timing	• When the feedback is given • How often the feedback is given	• Provide immediate feedback for content (right/wrong). • Delay feedback slightly for more mathematical practices and science and engineering practices. • Never delay feedback beyond when it would make a difference in students' learning in the moment. • Provide feedback as often as is practical for all processes, tasks, and products.	

CONTINUED

CONTINUED

FEEDBACK STRATEGIES CAN VARY IN TERMS OF . . .	IN THESE WAYS . . .	EXAMPLES AND THINGS TO CONSIDER	HOW CAN WE INCORPORATE PEER-TO-PEER FEEDBACK?
Amount	• How many feedback points? • How much information in each point?	• Focus on those points that are directly related to the success criteria. • Choose those points that are essential for closing the gap. • Take into account the developmental stage of the learner (e.g., kindergarteners compared to high school seniors).	
Mode	• Oral • Written • Visual/demonstration	• Select the best mode for the message. • When possible, it is best to engage in dialogue and questioning with the learner. • Give written feedback on written work. • Use teacher or student modeling if "how to do something" is an issue or if the student needs an example.	
Audience	• Individual • Group/class	• Individual feedback says, "The teacher values my learning." • Group/class feedback works if most of the learners need the feedback. If not, group/class feedback is not effective. • Would it suffice to make a comment when passing the learners as they work on a problem or experiment? • Is a one-on-one conference better for providing feedback?	

Let's look at specific examples of each of the variables in feedback to better see how this would look in our classrooms.

YOUR TURN!

Consider the following scenarios. With your colleagues, identify which one is more effective and why.

OPTION 1	OPTION 2	WHY?
A math teacher models four ways to solve a quadratic equation: graphing, completing the square, using the quadratic formula, and factoring. After each method or approach is presented, learners use that approach to solve a problem on their miniature whiteboards. They compare their solutions with a neighbor, discuss the problem-solving process, and evaluate the pros and cons of the strategy. As an exit ticket, they choose one strategy to solve a novel problem, defend their choice of strategy, and include questions they're wondering about.	The teacher works out multiple problems during the class period while students copy notes. Next, learners work in partners or alone to start their homework: problems 19–39 on page 263.	
As the teacher presents information on cell reproduction (mitosis and meiosis), she stops after each phase and asks learners to turn to a partner and summarize the specific phase. The partners then write summaries in their interactive notebooks. Finally, they pair with another pair to share summaries and check for differences, misconceptions, and questions. Before leaving class, they provide the teacher with a collective summary from their group of four with questions and misconceptions they may still have and would like addressed in the next day's lesson.	The teacher presents all phases of cell reproduction to students. For homework, learners must answer questions at the end of the chapter. The next day, she collects the homework to be graded by the next class period.	
An elementary teacher reads student writing samples and identifies common errors. She plans whole-class instruction on the use of reasons to support opinions because nearly every student in the class has neglected to do so. She also plans small-group lessons for students who had other errors in their writing, including tense, subject-verb agreement, or the lack of a clear opinion.	The teacher reads student work and provides written feedback to students. Students are expected to review the feedback and revise their papers accordingly.	
A history teacher uses an online game to quiz students. He displays a question and students select their response on their mobile phones. He then shows them the number of students who selected each option, asking them to talk with their partners about the data. He then invites students to respond to the question again before showing them the correct answer and asking them to discuss why the incorrect answers are not appropriate.	A history teacher gives a weekly quiz on Fridays and students receive their results on Mondays. They take a cumulative test at the end of the unit.	

The key difference between each of the four examples is the availability of timely feedback for content. Furthermore, Option 1 in each scenario suggests that the teacher was setting up the learning experience for learners to give and receive feedback at multiple points in the lesson. These multiple points are identified by the success criteria. In other words, the teachers in Option 1 offered the opportunity to give and receive feedback as learners progressed from one success criterion to the next.

Information about learners' performance within a specific timeframe allows them to use the information for improvement. Without timely information, learners cannot know where to go next and often continue moving forward, even if they are going in the wrong direction. But are there scenarios where delaying feedback is valuable in developing learners who can self-monitor, self-reflect, and self-evaluate? The answer is yes.

We hinted at this in the table on page 183. For example, delaying feedback can be helpful by providing students with opportunities to engage in the analysis of their own work (Butler, Karpicke, & Roediger, 2007). However, without scaffolding and support for doing this (e.g., single-point rubrics, analytic/holistic rubrics, co-constructed success criteria), positive gains disappear. On the other hand, immediate feedback produces significant gains when learners need that information to make corrective modifications during the deliberate practice of content (Eggen & Kauchak, 2004). In other words, immediate feedback on the current mathematics problem allows learners to adjust their approach to solving subsequent problems. Current feedback on their stoichiometry problems, understanding of the text, angular momentum calculations, summary of information, accuracy of timelines, or forced-choice environmental science homework allows learners to make an immediate adjustment (i.e., self-monitor, self-reflect, and self-evaluate) to their learning.

YOUR TURN!

Consider the following scenarios. With your colleagues, identify which one is more effective and why.

OPTION 1	OPTION 2	WHY?
A teacher confers with students as they work on a problem-solving set of rational expressions. He asks individual students and pairs of students what they are working on. Listening to the students' thinking allows him to make a decision about how to respond in that moment. The teacher refers to his planned questions, anticipated student strategies, and the success criteria to choose his response.	A teacher collects a problem-solving set on rational expressions. He marks which answers are not correct and returns the problem-solving set to learners at the end of the week.	
A teacher marks the incorrect solutions in a problem-solving set on balancing equations and returns the set to learners at the end of the week. She asks them to partner up and identify where they made mistakes in each incorrect solution. They are to describe, in their own words, how they would solve the problem differently in the future.	A teacher returns a problem-solving set on balancing equations to learners at the end of the week. She informs the students that these problems will be on the final test and they should review this set prior to taking the test.	

OPTION 1	OPTION 2	WHY?
A teacher listens to students read in a small group and notes errors in decoding. He pauses individual students as they read to support their decoding of specific words. He also provides direct instruction at the end of the lesson to all the students in the group based on the fact that they did not correctly decode words with the -ai pattern.	A teacher provides lessons to all students on -ai words because several students struggled with reading those words on their benchmark assessment. He also has students complete worksheets with a number of patterns for the /a/ sound.	
A teacher uses a vocabulary journal in her middle school social studies class. Students are expected to collect words that are unfamiliar to them as they listen, read, or view content. They then work in pairs to determine the meanings of the words. Sometimes all the students include a word and other times only some of the students add a term to their journals, depending on their knowledge base. The teacher uses this information to engage students in discussions and writing tasks.	A teacher gives students a list of words to learn. They are expected to define each term and demonstrate their understanding on quizzes and tests.	

Effective feedback must be specific to the success criteria. The feedback must also be specific about what additional steps will close the gap between where learners are and where they are going.

Comparing and contrasting the above examples, Option 1 provides specific information to learners that relates to the learning. Learners could use the information in Option 1 to identify how they were going and where they needed to go next in their learning. Students then have information that allows them to mind the learning gap. In addition,

Option 1 is constructive feedback. You may also have noticed that all the Option 1 scenarios were constructive. By being constructive, feedback serves a very useful purpose: *moving learning forward*. If the goal in each of our schools and classrooms is growth and achievement in learning, constructive feedback supports students as they progress in their learning. Growth implies that not all of our students may be where they need to be today, but they are further along today than they were yesterday. Constructive feedback makes the journey about learning, not the individual.

YOUR TURN!

Review three things described in this section that are needed for feedback to work. In our schools and classrooms, grades and feedback are used interchangeably. Is that appropriate? Use the following blank Venn diagram to compare and contrast feedback with grades.

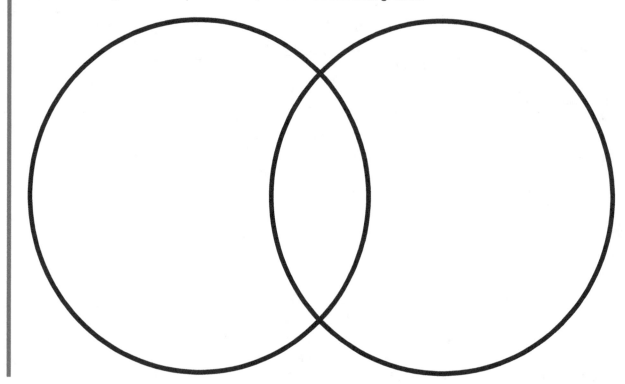

Now that you have finished this module, rate yourself on each of the following success criteria using the four-item scale. Use the space provided at the end to self-reflect on your own learning. What will you do next with this information? You may not yet be at the expert level, as it takes time to integrate knowledge into practice. Use this information to identify areas of continued learning.

- I can compare teacher feedback, student feedback, and self-feedback.

- I can describe the role of success criteria in structuring feedback.

- I can describe features of feedback that impact learning.

- I can distinguish between more and less effective feedback.

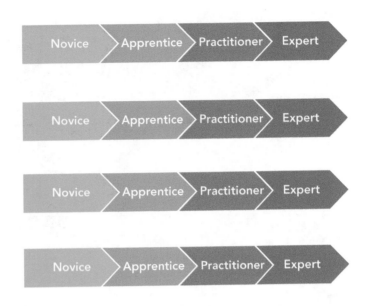

NOTES

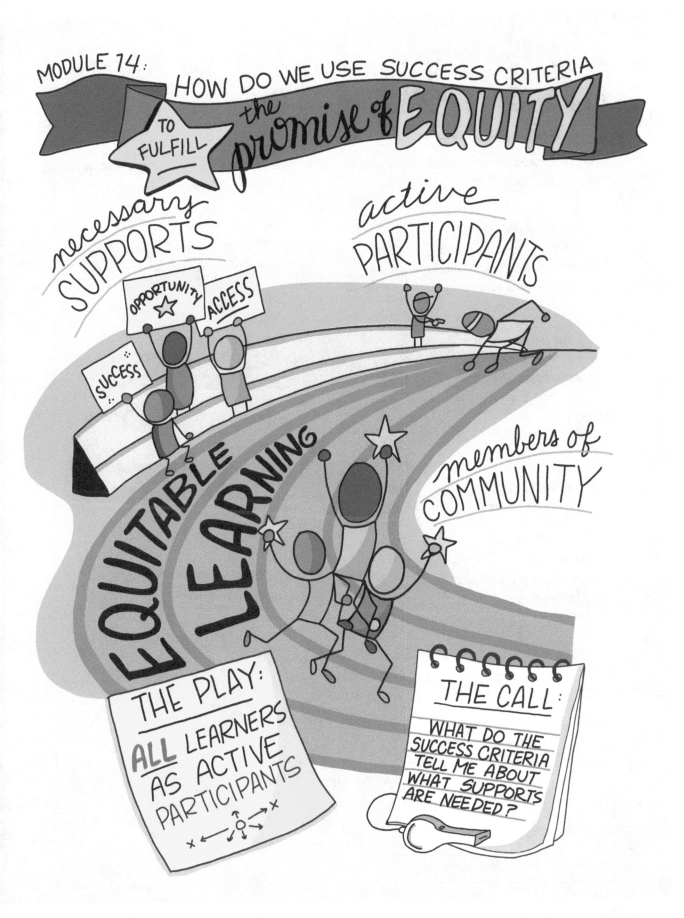

MODULE 14
HOW DO WE USE SUCCESS CRITERIA TO FULFILL THE PROMISE OF EQUITY?

Before you engage with the information in this module, rate yourself on each of the following success criteria using the four-item scale:

- I can describe the ways in which success criteria can promote equity and opportunities to learn.

- I can identify verbs in success criteria that indicate the skills all students must develop.

- I can design different means of engaging, representing, and expressing learning.

- I can identify compensatory and adaptive approaches that increase students' access to success.

The foundation of equity in our classrooms is the assurance that all learners will have access to high-quality teaching and learning and opportunities to learn. This requires that every learner is

- an active participant in his or her learning,

- accepted by others as an essential member of the classroom community, and

- Given the necessary supports that offer them the opportunity for success. (Jimenez et al., 2012; Spooner et al., 2011)

High-quality success criteria provide a pathway to equitable learning by offering clarity about how learners will show what they know.

YOUR TURN!

Return to Module 4 and the characteristics of high-quality *I can/We can* statements (see page 61). We will need to reference these characteristics as we look at how to use success criteria to promote equity.

ACTIVE AND ACCEPTED

The characteristics "actionable" and "focus on learning" are where we will start. Consider the following sets of success criteria first introduced in Module 4.

MATHEMATICS

I can explain the difference between a rational and an irrational number.

I can collaborate to name irrational numbers and estimate their approximate locations on a number line using rational numbers as benchmarks.

SCIENCE

I can identify each of the three types of rocks.

I can describe how their properties provide evidence of how they were formed.

ENGLISH LANGUAGE ARTS

I can identify the structure of a text using signal words. I can use signal words to identify the structure of a text.

I can compare a fictional account and a historical account of the same period to see how authors use or alter history.

HISTORY/SOCIAL STUDIES

I can describe contributions from Muslim scholars in the areas of science and medicine.

I can tell and show how land is used in urban, suburban, and rural areas.

The verbs in the success criteria describe the action associated with the learning. Therefore, the success criteria establish what **all** learners will do as active participants in this learning and as active members of the classroom community. In these examples, the verbs for math are *explain* and *collaborate*. For science, *identify* and *describe*. For English language arts, *identify* and *compare*. And for history, *tell*, *show*, and *describe*. This means we must expect and support all learners in the classroom in their explaining, collaborating, identifying, describing, comparing, and telling and showing. So, how do we make this happen?

To ensure equity of access and opportunity to learning, we have to provide learners with multiple means for engaging, representing, and expressing their learning (CAST, 2018). These means should take into account individuals' backgrounds and demographic characteristics, personal dispositions, and unique profiles. If we only provide a single means by which learners explain (e.g., writing), we will likely, even if unintentionally, exclude those learners who have barriers to writing (e.g., dyslexia, fine

> If we only provide a single means by which learners explain (e.g., writing), we will likely, even if unintentionally, exclude those learners who have barriers to writing.

motor challenges, language processing disability, developing knowledge of the English language, even lack of interest) from becoming active members of the classroom community. If we only provide a single means by which learners collaborate (e.g., ability grouping or with an instructional aide), then we limit the opportunity for any learner to fully be accepted as an essential member of the community.

YOUR TURN!

One of the first steps in using success criteria to promote equity of access and opportunity for learning is to develop multiple ways of accessing, building, and internalizing the learning. This means using multiple senses and modalities, different types of materials, and a variety of processes and products. With your colleagues, return to the list of what learners would say and do if they have mastered the learning intentions in Module 4 on page 61. Then, list multiple means for engaging, representing, and expressing their learning through the success criteria.

LEARNING INTENTIONS	EXAMPLES OF SUCCESS CRITERIA	DIFFERENT MEANS OF ENGAGING, REPRESENTING, AND EXPRESSING LEARNING
Mathematics		
We are learning about the role of irrational numbers within the number system.	• I can **explain** the difference between a rational and an irrational number. • I can **collaborate** to name irrational numbers and estimate their approximate locations on a number line using rational numbers as benchmarks.	***Explain and Collaborate:*** Learners can sketch and label, create a graphic organizer, talk with a peer, use language frames and cue cards, build with models and physical number lines on the floor, or compose a written, spoken-word, or charade response. Learners can take turns or work simultaneously to create one product, they can create separate products while talking and sharing ideas, or they can create products individually and then exchange them for feedback and revisions.

CONTINUED

CONTINUED

LEARNING INTENTIONS	EXAMPLES OF SUCCESS CRITERIA	DIFFERENT MEANS OF ENGAGING, REPRESENTING, AND EXPRESSING LEARNING
Science		
We are learning about the role of energy transfer in the rock cycle.	• We can **identify** each of the three types of rocks. • We can **descrtibe** how their properties provide evidence of how they were formed.	***Identify and Describe:*** Learners can do this in several ways: verbally, with partners, with groups of three, in writing, using cue or response cards with pictures or translated words, pointing, kinesthetically with samples, or using assistive technology (talker, iPad, etc.).

LEARNING INTENTIONS	EXAMPLES OF SUCCESS CRITERIA	DIFFERENT MEANS OF ENGAGING, REPRESENTING, AND EXPRESSING LEARNING
English Language Arts		
I am learning about informational text structures.	• I can use signal words to **identify** the structure of a text. • I can **explain** the characteristics of common types of text structures. • I can **use** my knowledge about text structure to organize my notes.	**Identify, Explain, and Use:** Students are provided with lists of signal words commonly used in different text structures. They review authentic mentor texts for the author's use of signal words. They meet with peers to identify the common characteristics of the different text structures before explaining the characteristics to their teacher during individual conferences. Students take notes about text structures and how they can use their knowledge to predict how the text will work. They then write a short informational essay using a text structure of their choice.

CONTINUED

CONTINUED

LEARNING INTENTIONS	EXAMPLES OF SUCCESS CRITERIA	DIFFERENT MEANS OF ENGAGING, REPRESENTING, AND EXPRESSING LEARNING
Social Studies		
We are learning about the contributions of Muslim scholars and their impact on later civilizations.	• We can **describe** contributions from Muslim scholars in the areas of science and medicine. • We can **describe** contributions from Muslim scholars in the areas of philosophy, art, and literature. • We can **describe** contributions from Muslim scholars in the area of mathematics.	*Describe:* Students can select informational sources (texts, videos, audio files) that provide them with information about Muslim scholars. They organize their notes using graphic organizers and concept maps. They can discuss ideas with peers and meet with their teacher in small groups as they develop their projects, which could be a short video, a podcast, a poster, or a written response. Each format requires that they describe some contributions of Muslim scholars. They then gallery walk and learn from their peers, asking questions they have prepared in advance.

Hopefully, the list you compiled in the last column included many different ways for learners to engage in the learning. For the examples provided, there are lots of different ways to explain, collaborate, identify, use, and describe. By developing multiple means for engaging, representing, and expressing learning, we create a classroom community in which every learner can find a way to successfully engage, represent, and express their learning. This is how we ensure they are an active participant in their learning and accepted by others as essential members of the classroom community.

PROVIDING THE NECESSARY SUPPORTS

High-quality success criteria can help provide the necessary supports that offer learners the opportunity for success. Consider the examples from the start of this module. The actions and the learning captured by the success criteria tell us what needs to be supported through compensatory or adaptive approaches. If learners are to explain and collaborate, what supports do we provide to ensure that they have the opportunity to explain and collaborate in their learning? Similarly, how do we provide supports for identifying and describing? Let's first define compensatory and adaptive approaches.

> The actions and the learning captured by the success criteria tell us what needs to be supported through compensatory or adaptive approaches.

COMPENSATORY APPROACHES

Compensatory approaches are additional supports designed to build on learners' strengths and, at the same time, address any barriers that may impede their ability to engage, represent, or express their learning. The level of complexity in the learning (e.g., the cognitive level of the verb) is held constant and not lessened or watered down with these approaches. Let's return to the previous examples. With compensatory approaches, learners are expected to *explain*, *collaborate*, *identify*, *use*, and *describe*. Students may need audio versions, additional wait time, sentence frames, additional prompting, or other supports that allow them to master the content. For example, a student learning about land forms may need visuals to understand the differences, whereas another student may benefit from a short video clip and still another might find a visualization useful.

ADAPTIVE APPROACHES

Adaptive approaches are additional supports that serve to accommodate or modify learning intentions and success criteria. Accommodations don't substantially change either of these for students, but instead they are designed to improve access to those opportunities. Accommodations can include changes to testing and assessment materials, access to assistive and adaptive technology, adaptations in the physical environment or in how information is presented, and alterations to timing and scheduling for the benefit of the learner. On the other hand, modifications are more significant adaptations and involve decisions that alter the learning intentions and success criteria. Modifications are reserved for students with more significant disabilities.

YOUR TURN!

Take a moment to return to the chart in the Your Turn! on page 193. Identify the different means for engaging, representing, and expressing learning that are also compensatory and/or adaptive approaches. List those in the space provided. (To note, some things in the third column are neither one).

COMPENSATORY APPROACHES	ADAPTIVE APPROACHES

Although there are times when modifications are required, ensuring that all learners have access and opportunity to the highest level of complexity is a key part of equity in the classroom. Remember, for compensatory approaches, the level of complexity must remain unchanged. Instead, we are providing supports that remove barriers not directly related to the learning intention and success criteria. To be very direct, if English is not the learner's primary language, this does not mean she does not have the capacity to explain or collaborate. We must offer supports that allow the learner to engage, represent, and express her learning. Likewise, if a learner has a disability that interferes with his ability to communicate verbally, we must offer supports that allow him to identify and describe by some other means. The learner's ability to communicate verbally is not related to his capacity to understand the transfer of energy in the rock cycle and then describe that transfer.

So to review, the success criteria, by their very definition, define for us that learners should have equity of access and opportunity to learning because they are

- active participants in their learning,
- accepted by others as essential members of the classroom community, and
- Given the necessary supports that offer them the opportunity for success. (Jimenez et al., 2012; Spooner et al., 2011)

Through the success criteria, we now know what *active* looks like, we know what *accepted* looks like, and we can accurately and precisely identify and implement supports that allow **all** learners the chance to be successful.

> Ensuring that all learners have access and opportunity to the highest level of complexity is a key part of equity in the classroom.

YOUR TURN!

Take one final look at the compensatory approaches and the means for engaging, representing, and expressing learning in the third column of the chart on page 191. Ensure that the means align with the cognitive level of the verbs in the success criteria.

Now you are ready to create and share high-quality success criteria that maximize learning for all students! Together, let's support them in hitting the target.

Now that you have finished this module, rate yourself on each of the following success criteria using the four-item scale. Use the space provided at the end to self-reflect on your own learning. What will you do next with this information? You may not yet be at the expert level, as it takes time to integrate knowledge into practice. Use this information to identify areas of continued learning.

- I can describe the ways in which success criteria can promote equity and opportunities to learn.

- I can identify verbs in success criteria that indicate the skills all students must develop.

- I can design different means of engaging, representing, and expressing learning.

- I can identify compensatory and adaptive approaches that increase students' access to success.

REFERENCES

Brookhart, S. M. (2008). *How to give effective feedback to your students*. Alexandria, VA: ASCD.

Brookhart, S. M. (2013). *How to create and use rubrics for formative assessment and grading*. Alexandria, VA: ASCD.

Butler, A. C., Karpicke, J. D., & Roediger, H. L. (2007). The effect of type and timing of feedback on learning from multiple-choice tests. *Journal of Experimental Psychology: Applied, 13*, 273–281.

California Department of Education. (2019). *Historical and social sciences analysis skills*. Retrieved from https://www.cde.ca.gov/be/st/ss/hssanalysisskills.asp

CAST. (2018). *Universal Design for Learning guidelines, version 2.2*. Retrieved from http://udlguidelines.cast.org

Eggen, P., & Kauchak, D. (2004). *Educational psychology: Windows on classrooms* (6th ed). Columbus, OH: Prentice Hall.

Ericsson, K. A. (2008). Deliberate practice and acquisition of expert performance: A general overview. *Academic Emergency Medicine, 15*, 988–994.

Ericsson, K. A., Krampe, R. T., & Tesch-Romer, C. (1993). The role of deliberate practice in the acquisition of expert performance. *Psychological Review, 100*, 363–406.

Ericsson, K. A., & Pool, R. (2016). *Peak: Secrets from the new science of expertise*. New York, NY: Houghton Mifflin Harcourt.

Feltz, D. L., Short, S. E., & Sullivan, P. J. (2008). *Self-efficacy in sport*. Champaign, IL: Human Kinetics.

Fennell, F. S., Kobett, B. M., & Wray, J. A. (2017). *The formative 5: Everyday assessment techniques for every math classroom*. Thousand Oaks, CA: Corwin.

Fisher, D., Frey, N., Almarode, J., Flories, K., & Nagel, D. (2020). *PLC+: Better decisions and greater impact by design*. Thousand Oaks, CA: Corwin.

Fisher, D., Frey, N., Amador, O., & Assof, J. (2019). *The teacher clarity playbook: A hands-on guide to creating learning intentions and success criteria for organized, effective instruction*. Thousand Oaks, CA: Corwin.

Florida Department of Education. (2019). *Florida's B.E.S.T. standards: English language arts*. Tallahassee, FL: Author.

Frey, N., Hattie, J., & Fisher, D. (2018). *Developing assessment-capable visible learners, Grades K–12: Maximizing skill, will and thrill*. Thousand Oaks, CA: Corwin.

Harmon, P. (1968). A classification of performance objective behaviors in job training programs. *Educational Technology, 8*(22), 11–16.

Hattie, J. A. (2012). *Visible learning for teachers: Maximizing impact on teachers*. New York, NY: Routledge.

Jimenez, B., Browder, D., Spooner, F., & DiBiase, W. (2012). Inclusive inquiry science using peer-mediated embedded instruction for students with moderate intellectual disability. *Exceptional Children, 78*, 301–317.

Merriam-Webster. (1999). *Merriam-Webster's collegiate dictionary* (10th ed.). Springfield, MA: Author.

Merriam-Webster. (2020a). Equity. In *Merriam-Webster.com dictionary*. Retrieved from https://www.merriam-webster.com/dictionary/equity

Merriam-Webster. (2020b). Playbook. In *Merriam-Webster.com dictionary*. Retrieved from https://www.merriam-webster.com/dictionary/playbook

National Governors Association Center for Best Practices & Council of Chief State School Officers. (2010). *Common Core State Standards for Mathematics*. Washington, DC: Author.

National Research Council. (2013). *Next Generation Science Standards: For states, by states*. Washington, DC: National Academies Press.

Spooner, F., Knight, V., Browder, D. M., Jimenez, B., & DiBiase, W. (2011). Evaluating evidence-based practice in teaching science content to students with severe developmental disabilities. *Research and Practice for Persons With Severe Disabilities, 36*, 62–75.

Visible Learning Meta[X]. (2020, May). Retrieved from https://www.visiblelearningmetax.com/

Wiggins, G., & McTighe, J. (2005). *Understanding by design* (2nd ed.). Alexandria, VA: ASCD.

INDEX

A SAGE Publishing Company

CORWIN HAS ONE MISSION: to enhance education through intentional professional learning.

We build long-term relationships with our authors, educators, clients, and associations who partner with us to develop and continuously improve the best evidence-based practices that establish and support lifelong learning.

CORWIN Fisher & Frey

> **Every student deserves a great teacher—not by chance, but by design.**

Read more from Fisher & Frey

Catapult teachers beyond learning intentions to clearly define what success looks like for every student. Designed to be used collaboratively in grade-level, subject-area teams—or even on your own—the step-by-step playbook expands teacher understanding of how success criteria can be utilized to maximize student learning.

Disrupt the cycle of implicit bias and stereotype threat with 40 research-based, teacher-tested techniques; individual, classroom-based, and schoolwide actions; printables; and ready-to-go tools for planning and instruction.

Explore a new model of reading instruction that goes beyond teaching skills to fostering engagement and motivation. *Comprehension* is the structured framework you need to empower students to comprehend text and take action in the world.

When you increase your credibility with students, student motivation rises. And when you partner with other teachers to achieve this, students learn more. This playbook illuminates the connection between teacher credibility and collective efficacy and offers specific actions educators can take to improve both.

Tap your intuition, collaborate with your peers, and put the research-based strategies embedded in this road map to work in your classroom to implement or deepen a strong and successful balanced literacy program.

With cross-curricular examples, planning templates, professional learning questions, and a PLC guide, this is the most practical planner for designing and delivering highly effective instruction.

To order your copies, visit corwin.com/FisherandFrey